Computer Science Experiments

FACTS ON FILE SCIENCE EXPERIMENTS

Computer Science Experiments

Pamela Walker
Elaine Wood

Facts On File
An imprint of Infobase Publishing

Computer Science Experiments

Text and artwork copyright © 2010 by Infobase Publishing

Editor: Frank K. Darmstadt
Copy Editor for A Good Thing, Inc.: Betsy Feist
Project Coordination: Aaron Richman
Art Director: Howard Petlack
Production: Victoria Kessler
Illustrations: Hadel Studios

Facts On File, Inc.
An imprint of Infobase Publishing
132 West 31st Street
New York NY 10001

Library of Congress Cataloging-in-Publication Data
Walker, Pam, 1958-
Computer science experiments / Pamela Walker, Elaine Wood.
p. cm.—(Facts on File science experiments)
Includes bibliographical references and index.
ISBN 978-0-8160-7806-6
1. Computer science–Experiments–Juvenile literature. 2. Computer science–Study and teaching–Juvenile literature. I. Wood, Elaine, 1950- II. Title.
QA76.27.W34 2009
004.07–dc22
2009010704

Facts On File books are available at special discounts when purchased in bulk quantities for businesses, associations, institutions, or sales promotions. Please call our Special Sales Department in New York at 212/967-8800 or 800/322-8755.

You can find Facts On File on the World Wide Web at http://www.factsonfile.com

Printed in the United States of America

Bang AGT 10 9 8 7 6 5 4 3 2 1

This book is printed on acid-free paper.

Contents

Preface

For centuries, humans have studied and explored the natural world around them. The ever-growing body of knowledge resulting from these efforts is science. Information gained through science is passed from one generation to the next through an array of educational programs. One of the primary goals of every science education program is to help young people develop critical-thinking and problem-solving skills that they can use throughout their lives.

Science education is unique in academics in that it not only conveys facts and skills; it also cultivates curiosity and creativity. For this reason, science is an active process that cannot be fully conveyed by passive teaching techniques. The question for educators has always been, "What is the best way to teach science?" There is no simple answer to this question, but studies in education provide useful insights.

Research indicates that students need to be actively involved in science, learning it through experience. Science students are encouraged to go far beyond the textbook and to ask questions, consider novel ideas, form their own predictions, develop experiments or procedures, collect information, record results, analyze findings, and use a variety of resources to expand knowledge. In other words, students cannot just hear science; they must also do science.

"Doing" science means performing experiments. In the science curriculum, experiments play a number of educational roles. In some cases, hands-on activities serve as hooks to engage students and introduce new topics. For example, a discrepant event used as an introductory experiment encourages questions and inspires students to seek the answers behind their findings. Classroom investigations can also help expand information that was previously introduced or cement new knowledge. According to neuroscience, experiments and other types of hands-on learning help transfer new learning from short-term into long-term memory.

Facts On File Science Experiments is a six-volume set of experiments that helps engage students and enable them to "do" science. The high-interest experiments in these books put students' minds into gear and give them opportunities to become involved, to think independently, and to build on their own base of science knowledge.

As a resource, Facts On File Science Experiments provides teachers with new and innovative classroom investigations that are presented in a clear, easy-to-understand style. The areas of study in the six-volume set include forensic science, environmental science, computer research, physical science, weather and climate, and space and astronomy. Experiments are supported by colorful figures and line illustrations that help hold students' attention and explain information. All of the experiments in these books use multiple science process skills such as observing, measuring, classifying, analyzing, and predicting. In addition, some of the experiments require students to practice inquiry science by setting up and carrying out their own open-ended experiments.

Each volume of the set contains 20 new experiments as well as extensive safety guidelines, glossary, correlation to the National Science Education Standards, scope and sequence, and an annotated list of Internet resources. An introduction that presents background information begins each investigation to provide an overview of the topic. Every experiment also includes relevant specific safety tips along with materials list, procedure, analysis questions, explanation of the experiment, connections to real life, and an annotated further reading section for extended research.

Pam Walker and Elaine Wood, the authors of Facts On File Science Experiments, are sensitive to the needs of both science teachers and students. The writing team has more than 40 years of combined science teaching experience. Both are actively involved in planning and improving science curricula in their home state, Georgia, where Pam was the 2007 Teacher of the Year. Walker and Wood are master teachers who hold specialist degrees in science and science education. They are the authors of dozens of books for middle and high school science teachers and students.

Facts On File Science Experiments, by Walker and Wood, facilitates science instruction by making it easy for teachers to incorporate experimentation. During experiments, students reap benefits that are not available in other types of instruction. One of these benefits is the opportunity to take advantage of the learning provided by social interactions. Experiments are usually carried out in small groups, enabling students to brainstorm and learn from each other. The validity of group work as an effective learning tool is supported by research in neuroscience, which shows that the brain is a social organ and that communication and collaboration are activities that naturally enhance learning.

Experimentation addresses many different types of learning, including lateral thinking, multiple intelligences, and constructivism. In lateral thinking, students solve problems using nontraditional methods. Long-established, rigid procedures for problem-solving are replaced by original ideas from students. When encouraged to think laterally, students are more likely to come up with unique ideas that are not usually found in the traditional classroom. This type of thinking requires students to construct meaning from an activity and to think like scientists.

Another benefit of experimentation is that it accommodates students' multiple intelligences. According to the theory of multiple intelligences, students possess many different aptitudes, but in varying degrees. Some of these forms of intelligence include linguistic, musical, logical-mathematical, spatial, kinesthetic, intrapersonal, and interpersonal. Learning is more likely to be acquired and retained when more than one sense is involved. During an experiment, students of all intellectual types find roles in which they can excel.

Students in the science classroom become involved in active learning, constructing new ideas based on their current knowledge and their experimental findings. The constructivist theory of learning encourages students to discover principles for and by themselves. Through problem solving and independent thinking, students build on what they know, moving forward in a manner that makes learning real and lasting.

Active, experimental learning makes connections between newly acquired information and the real world, a world that includes jobs. In the twenty-first century, employers expect their employees to identify and solve problems for themselves. Therefore, today's students, workers of the near future, will be required to use higher-level thinking skills. Experience with science experiments provides potential workers with the ability and confidence to be problem solvers.

The goal of Walker and Wood in Facts On File Science Experiments is to provide experiments that hook and hold the interest of students, teach basic concepts of science, and help students develop their critical-thinking skills. When fully immersed in an experiment, students can experience those "Aha!" moments, the special times when new information merges with what is already known and understanding breaks through. On these occasions, real and lasting learning takes place. The authors hope that this set of books helps bring more "Aha" moments into every science class.

Acknowledgments

This book would not exist were it not for our editor, Frank K. Darmstadt, who conceived and directed the project. Frank supervised the material closely, editing and making invaluable comments along the way. Betsy Feist of A Good Thing, Inc., is responsible for transforming our raw material into a polished and grammatically correct manuscript that makes us proud.

Introduction

In the mid-1990s, the personal computer began to make its way into the classroom. Initially, most classrooms had only one computer, which was primarily used by teachers for record keeping. From the late 1990s until today, the number of computers in schools has increased at a rate faster than predicted by experts, and many classrooms have 10 or more Internet-ready units available for student use. The advent of computers in schools has had a tremendous impact on the way instruction is delivered.

In science classrooms, computers can stimulate learning in many ways. Computers can be tools for engaging students because they grab and hold student interest. Once a student is "hooked," a computer with Internet access can help cement learning because it is an interactive device that engages the brain and leads the student to ask "how" and "why" questions. Active learning often makes education more fun and interesting and increases the chance that knowledge acquired will be retained. In addition, the Internet brings into classrooms virtual activities that are too dangerous, too expensive, or too complex to actually carry out. Using the computer, a student can see some of the millions of practical applications of science theory, a view that often awakens curiosity. Computers in classrooms also foster positive attitudes toward learning science and stimulate interest in science concepts.

Access to the Internet makes computers especially useful. Research, which is natural and integral part of science, was one of the reasons the Internet was created. The Internet was developed in the 1980s by the National Science Foundation to facilitate the sharing of information between scientists. Today, this scientific information is available to students, teachers, parents, and others. Computer use and Internet access make it possible for students to model the behavior of real scientists, who rely on the Internet for tasks such as gathering and analyzing data and carrying out research.

Since its beginning, the nature of the Internet has changed dramatically. Once a source of shared scientific information, today's Internet hosts content posted by people from every walk of life. Although the collection of scientific information has grown, so has the pool of material inappropriate students and other young researchers. Internet use should always be supervised by adults.

Real scientists carry out research to provide background information on experimental topics as well as to develop new ideas for future experiments. Ideally, research reveals both historically important information and the newest work of scientists from around the world. Students and teachers know that very little research can be done in a science classroom using the traditional textbooks. Access to the Internet broadens students' exposure to accomplishments and ideas. The Internet also makes it possible for students to gather data in real time. This data can be used as a basis for experimentation or for analysis.

Computer Science Experiments offers 20 engaging experiments and activities based on computer research. Some of the experiments also require students to build models or perform experiments. This volume is part of the new Facts On File Science Experiments multivolume set.

The experiments in this volume come from all major areas of science, including biology, environmental science, physics, chemistry, and Earth systems. Experiments based on biological principles include "Bioethics Video Production," in which students learn about the complexity of bioethical topics, then work in small groups to explore one issue and produce a short video explaining it. "Virtual Fetal Pig Dissection" is an ideal activity for classrooms that cannot afford preserved fetal pigs and dissecting equipment or for students who have objections to dissection. "Human Parasites" introduces students to the types of parasites that infect people, the complex life cycles of parasites, and the treatments for these pests. In "Breathing Demonstration," students must integrate an understanding of the mechanics of external respiration and the gas laws to develop a model that explains the movement of air into and out of the lungs.

The physical sciences, chemistry and physics, are the focus of several experiments. "Hydrolysis and Dehydration Synthesis" explains how large molecules, including those found in living things, combine and break apart. In this experiment, students also build and use models to demonstrate these chemical reactions. "Types of Chemical Bonds" examines the role of valence electrons in building molecules as well as the chemistry behind hydrogen bonding. "Conservation of Mass," an activity based on the work of Antoine-Laurent and Marie Anne Lavoisier, links the work of early scientists to today's body of knowledge. "Simple

Machines" offers teachers a new approach to presenting some basic concepts in a new and engaging way.

Lessons learned in environmental science are some of the most relevant in day-to-day life. In "Coral Reef Conservation," students explore the populations of reefs and look into the problems that human cause for these ecosystems. To closely examine their own impact on the environment, students calculate their environmental impact in "Carbon Footprint." This experiment helps students to identify the activities in their lives that most degrade the environment and to look at some options that reduce their impact. "The History of DDT" lets students find out how a "wonder chemical" led to significant environmental and population damage. Like "Bioethics Video Production," this laboratory incorporates the socioeconomic and medical aspects, helping students understand the complexities of the issues.

The study of Earth systems includes the planet's role in space, the science of space and space travel, conditions on the Earth, and the interactions of Earth with other objects in space. The surface of the Earth is the topic of two experiments. In "How Are Caves Formed?" students examine the differences in primary and secondary caves. "Rocks and Minerals" differentiates the two types of surface materials and lets students research a mineral of their choice. The Sun is the topic of "Sunspots and the Solar Cycle," an experiment that has students examine the most recent solar spot activity on the Sun's surface. "Astronaut Trading Cards" looks at the history of the space program, highlighting current work on the International Space Station. Climate and weather are explored in "Using Cloud Patterns to Predict Weather," "Create a Climatogram," and "Mapping Lightning Frequency." The physics of a tsunami, as well as the human impact of this type of storm, are examined in "The Power of a Tsunami."

By using the experiments in this book, teachers can cover key science concepts while expanding students' learning experiences. Without a doubt, students who are exposed to a variety of engaging learning styles are the ones who are most likely to find school fun and meaningful. Internet-based research naturally complements traditional science and helps students see how this tool can support their life-long learning.

Safety Precautions

REVIEW BEFORE STARTING ANY EXPERIMENT

Each experiment includes special safety precautions that are relevant to that particular project. These do not include all the basic safety precautions that are necessary whenever you are working on a scientific experiment. For this reason, it is absolutely necessary that you read and remain mindful of the General Safety Precautions that follow. Experimental science can be dangerous and good laboratory procedure always includes following basic safety rules. Things can happen quickly while you are performing an experiment—for example, materials can spill, break, or even catch on fire. There will not be time after the fact to protect yourself. Always prepare for unexpected dangers by following the basic safety guidelines during the entire experiment, whether or not something seems dangerous to you at a given moment.

We have been quite sparing in prescribing safety precautions for the individual experiments. For one reason, we want you to take very seriously the safety precautions that are printed in this book. If you see it written here, you can be sure that it is here because it is absolutely critical.

Read the safety precautions here and at the beginning of each experiment before performing each lab activity. It is difficult to remember a long set of general rules. By rereading these general precautions every time you set up an experiment, you will be reminding yourself that lab safety is critically important. In addition, use your good judgment and pay close attention when performing potentially dangerous procedures. Just because the book does not say "Be careful with hot liquids" or "Don't cut yourself with a knife" does not mean that you can be careless when boiling water or using a knife to punch holes in plastic bottles. Notes in the text are special precautions to which you must pay special attention.

GENERAL SAFETY PRECAUTIONS

Accidents can be caused by carelessness, haste, or insufficient knowledge. By practicing safety procedures and being alert while conducting experiments, you can avoid taking an unnecessary risk. Be sure to check the individual experiments in this book for additional safety regulations and adult supervision requirements. If you will be working in a laboratory, do not work alone. When you are working off site, keep in groups with a minimum of three students per group, and follow school rules and state legal requirements for the number of supervisors required. Ask an adult supervisor with basic training in first aid to carry a small first-aid kit. Make sure everyone knows where this person will be during the experiment.

PREPARING

- Clear all surfaces before beginning experiments.
- Read the entire experiment before you start.
- Know the hazards of the experiments and anticipate dangers.

PROTECTING YOURSELF

- Follow the directions step by step.
- Perform only one experiment at a time.
- Locate exits, fire blanket and extinguisher, master gas and electricity shut-offs, eyewash, and first-aid kit.
- Make sure there is adequate ventilation.
- Do not participate in horseplay.
- Do not wear open-toed shoes.
- Keep floor and workspace neat, clean, and dry.
- Clean up spills immediately.
- If glassware breaks, do not clean it up by yourself; ask for teacher assistance.
- Tie back long hair.
- Never eat, drink, or smoke in the laboratory or workspace.
- Do not eat or drink any substances tested unless expressly permitted to do so by a knowledgeable adult.

USING EQUIPMENT WITH CARE

- Set up apparatus far from the edge of the desk.
- Use knives or other sharp, pointed instruments with care.

- Pull plugs, not cords, when removing electrical plugs.
- Clean glassware before and after use.
- Check glassware for scratches, cracks, and sharp edges.
- Let your teacher know about broken glassware immediately.
- Do not use reflected sunlight to illuminate your microscope.
- Do not touch metal conductors.
- Take care when working with any form of electricity.
- Use alcohol-filled thermometers, not mercury-filled thermometers.

USING CHEMICALS

- Never taste or inhale chemicals.
- Label all bottles and apparatus containing chemicals.
- Read labels carefully.
- Avoid chemical contact with skin and eyes (wear safety glasses or goggles, lab apron, and gloves).
- Do not touch chemical solutions.
- Wash hands before and after using solutions.
- Wipe up spills thoroughly.

HEATING SUBSTANCES

- Wear safety glasses or goggles, apron, and gloves when heating materials.
- Keep your face away from test tubes and beakers.
- When heating substances in a test tube, avoid pointing the top of the test tube toward other people.
- Use test tubes, beakers, and other glassware made of Pyrex™ glass.
- Never leave apparatus unattended.
- Use safety tongs and heat-resistant gloves.
- If your laboratory does not have heatproof workbenches, put your Bunsen burner on a heatproof mat before lighting it.
- Take care when lighting your Bunsen burner; light it with the airhole closed and use a Bunsen burner lighter rather than wooden matches.

- Turn off hot plates, Bunsen burners, and gas when you are done.
- Keep flammable substances away from flames and other sources of heat.
- Have a fire extinguisher on hand.

FINISHING UP

- Thoroughly clean your work area and any glassware used.
- Wash your hands.
- Be careful not to return chemicals or contaminated reagents to the wrong containers.
- Do not dispose of materials in the sink unless instructed to do so.
- Clean up all residues and put in proper containers for disposal.
- Dispose of all chemicals according to all local, state, and federal laws.

BE SAFETY CONSCIOUS AT ALL TIMES!

1. Bioethics Video Production

Topic

Bioethical decision making requires an understanding of science and technology.

Introduction

Genetics is a fast-paced branch of science that is changing the way people think and live. Advances in the field of genetics, the branch of biology that deals with heredity, have opened new doors for experimentation and medical treatments that were unheard of in the not-so-distant past. Within the last 40 years, some of the milestone discoveries in genetics include locating segments of DNA that cause diseases, manipulating embryos, like the one shown in Figure 1, and growing stem cells.

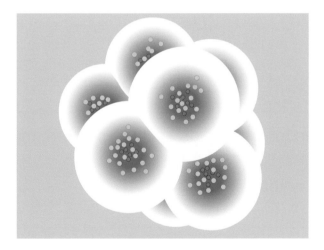

Figure 1

Embryo

With these medical advances, individuals are facing new and difficult questions. Many involve not only the new scientific knowledge but also the personal belief systems of individuals. For example, one tough topic that is still under debate is "Should parents be allowed to plan the genetic traits of their offspring?" Another complex issue is "Should *stem cells* be used to treat diseases?" If the answer to that question is "yes," then we must decide where to get those stem cells. Scientists are also still debating the matter of whether or not humans should be cloned. None of these questions are straightforward, and they may be debated for decades.

To address these matters, people need information on the science and technology involved. Knowledge of science gives individuals the tools required to analyze bioethical dilemmas. By understanding the science, one can weigh the consequences of their decisions against their moral beliefs. In this way, individuals can develop a course of action for themselves and their loved ones.

In this activity, you and your lab partners will conduct research on a controversial topic related to *bioethics*. You will present a short news broadcast on the science of the topic and explain the pros and cons of the issues involved.

Time Required

three or four 55-minute class periods

Materials

- ⚬ access to a video camera
- ⚬ access to a computer with word processor
- ⚬ access to the Internet
- ⚬ materials for visual aids such as posters, models, graphs, or charts
- ⚬ science notebook

Safety Note   **Please review and follow the safety guidelines at the beginning of this volume.**

Procedure

1. Work with your lab partners to research the topic assigned by your teacher. Conduct your research on the Internet. You may use any teacher-approved Web sites.

2. Once your group has completed its research, prepare and present a "news broadcast" on your assigned topic. To do so:

    a. Assign these roles in members of your group:

       ✔ host or interviewer

       ✔ guest who supports the pro side of a topic presented in your research

       ✔ guest who supports the con side of a topic presented in your research

      If the group is large enough, create other roles such as concerned citizens, parents of sick children, patients suffering from diseases, or legislators who are interested in the ethics of science.

    b. The host or interviewer should prepare four questions to ask each guest. Each guest will then answer the questions in a way that is scientifically correct and that completely explains his/her position on questions related to the topic.

    c. The host and guests may play the roles of real television hosts, science experts, or individuals who have opinions on the topic, or they may create fictitious roles. All members of the group should be prepared and know his/her material. During the presentation, notes can be used for reference, but they should not be read.

    d. Each member of the group should dress for his/her part.

    e. The interview questions and answers should be typed and turned in to the teacher on the day of the presentation.

    f. The group should film the news program with the video camera and turn in the video to the teacher on the due date. Alternatively, if no video camera is available, the program can be performed live.

    g. A visual aid should be included in the news broadcast. Appropriate visual aids include relevant posters, charts, graphs, tables, and models.

    h. The news broadcast should be creative and interesting.

    i. The news broadcast should last 5 to 10 minutes.

3. After you have researched the topic assigned to you and helped your group prepare the news broadcast, write a personal, one-page position paper on the topic. The paper should:

    a. Describe your personal views on the topic and explain how and why you arrived at those views.

    b. Include a bibliography that has three or more references.

4. On the day broadcasts are "aired" in class, listen to other groups' performances and take notes in your science notebook.

5. After the broadcasts, ask questions of the groups that produced them to help clarify you own understanding of these issues. Add the answers to the notes in your science notebook.

Analysis

1. Why are there more bioethical questions to be answered now than in the past?

2. What types of bioethical questions or topics concern you the most?

3. Why do you think that bioethical questions are complex and difficult to answer?

4. Scientists are able to treat some patients through gene therapy. In this technique, viruses are used to insert corrective genes into the DNA of patients. Some people believe that the manipulation of genes is contrary to the laws of nature. How do you feel about this topic?

5. A friend tells you that he has a serious genetic disease, but wants to keep it a secret so that he will not have trouble getting health insurance. What kind of advise would you give your friend?

What's Going On?

As science advances, bioethical questions will arise more frequently. The pace of technological discovery is picking up speed, creating an avalanche of new information, procedures, and possibilities. As a result, individuals and families will be forced to decide what is right and wrong for them personally. Unfortunately, the answers to many of these new dilemmas are difficult. Even well-informed people who are trying to do the right thing may disagree on what is right.

The number of bioethical issues will continue to grow. In the future, you may have to make both serious and mundane decisions. Are you in favor of undoing the effects of aging? What are your opinions on using embryos as sources of stem cells? Might you be willing to put up for adoption the frozen embryos that you and your spouse do not plan to use? In a restaurant, will you order salmon that have been genetically changed to grow extremely large (like the one in the top of Figure 2) or will you prefer the smaller, wild-type salmon? The more you know about the science behind these procedures, the better prepared you will be recognizing ethical dilemmas and for making the best decisions.

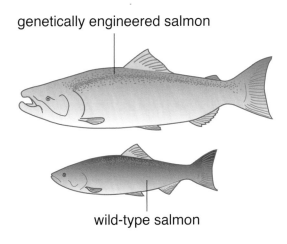

genetically engineered salmon

wild-type salmon

Figure 2

Connections

Medical science is devoted to preventing pain and disease. But is it ethical to prevent disease by permitting only healthy embryos to develop and survive? Doctors using a new technique, preimplantation genetic diagnosis (PGD), believe that it is. PGD is an offshoot of *in vitro fertilization*, a technique in which several eggs are removed from a woman's ovary and placed in petri dishes. The woman's partner donates sperm, which are mixed with the eggs. After several eggs are fertilized, a few are placed inside the woman's uterus, hoping that at least one will implant and develop into a healthy baby. In PGD, researchers examine the genetic material of the embryos before implantation. Fertilized eggs that carry genetic disorders are eliminated. Advocates point out that much suffering is avoided by implanting only the healthy eggs. Those who disagree say that this procedure is similar to breeding livestock and is unethical.

 Want to Know More?

See appendix for Our Findings.

Further Reading

Caplan, Arthur L. "Should Kids Be Conceived After a Parent Dies," Bioethics.net, Bioethics on MSNBC, June 27, 2007. Available online. URL: http://www.bioethics.net/articles.php?viewCat=2&articleId=196. Accessed July 8, 2008. The technology and questions behind using sperm of dead partners are explored in this article.

Highfield, Roger. "Human-Pig Hybrid Embryos Given Go Ahead," Telegraph. co.uk, January 7, 2008. Available online. URL: http://www.telegraph. co.uk/scienceandtechnology/science/sciencenews/3338904/Hybrids-separating-hope-from-hype.html. Accessed July 8, 2008. Highfield explains the reasons behind developing human-animal hybrids.

Sullivan, Dennis M. "Reproductive Technologies 101," Bioethics.com, February 14, 2007. Available online. URL: http://bioethics.com/?page_id=1733. Accessed July 8, 2008. Techniques behind embryo implantation are explained on this Web site.

2. Coral Reef Conservation

Topic

Coral reefs are complex ecosystems that are endangered by human activity.

Introduction

Coral reefs are some of the most colorful and diverse ecosystems on Earth. The structures of reefs are large and impressive, but the reef-building organisms are small *invertebrates* that are related to anemones and jellyfish, all members of the family *Cnidaria.* Coral animals rarely live alone. They form big groups called colonies in which the animals connect to each (see Figure 1).

Figure 1

Coral colony

Corals can be divided into two major types: soft and hard. Soft corals have flexible skeletons made of *gorgonin*, a tough protein. Scattered throughout the gorgonin are sharp *spicules* of calcium carbonate. Hard corals build a cup-shaped home of calcium carbonate. If threatened by predators, the animals pull themselves inside their protective skeletons. When hard corals die, their skeletons are left behind and become the base on which other corals build. Millions of coral skeletons form a reef.

Under ideal environmental conditions, coral reefs grow at the rate of about 3.9 inches (in.) (10 centimeters [cm.]) each year. For such growth to occur, the water must be clear so that light can penetrate. In addition, temperatures must range from 73.4 to 84.2 degrees Fahrenheit (°F) (23 to 29 degrees Celsius [°C]). The creation of a large reef can take thousands of years. Reefs around the world are having trouble surviving because of damage to the environment. In this activity, you will conduct research on coral reefs and learn how to help conserve these unique ecosystems.

Time Required

55 minutes for part A
55 minutes for part B

Materials

- ⚬ access to the Internet
- ⚬ colored pencils or markers
- ⚬ science notebook

Safety Note   Please review and follow the safety guidelines at the beginning of this volume.

Procedure, Part A

1. Access the following Web site: URL: http://oceanservice.noaa.gov/education/kits/corals/welcome.html.

2. Read through the Web site, using the "→" button to navigate forward. As you read, answer the Analysis questions.

3. Click on the image of a coral polyp to show a detailed, labeled diagram. Draw this diagram in your science notebook. Include all the labels.

4. Click on the image of a nematocyst to show a detailed, labeled diagram. Draw this diagram in your science notebook. Include all the labels.

5. Click on the image of a coral reef to show an enlarged diagram. Draw this diagram in your science notebook. Include all the labels.

Procedure, Part B

1. Many of the troubles facing coral reefs are caused by human activity. As you completed Part 1, you read about some of the problems. Select a problem and search the Internet for sites that suggest solutions to the problem. Read these sites and take notes in your science notebook. Write a 500-word paper on the problem and solution.

Analysis

1. What are three basic types of coral?
2. What is a coral polyp?
3. Why are corals described as *colonial organisms*?
4. How does a coral organism take in food? How does it get rid of wastes?
5. How do corals use nematocysts to capture their food?
6. Explain the mutualistic relationship between zooxanthellae and corals.
7. What is coral bleaching?
8. Why do coral require clear, nutrient-poor water?
9. How does a coral reef form?
10. Match the shapes of corals to their descriptions.

    _____ have large, flattened branches

    _____ have wide plates that create whorllike patterns

    _____ resemble fingers

    _____ grow in thin layers on the substrate

    a. encrusting coral
    b. elkhorn coral
    c. foliase coral
    d. digitate coral
11. How do coral reefs get started?
12. What are three types of coral reefs?
13. How long does it take for barrier reefs to fully form?
14. What type of environment is best for reef-building corals?
15. Why are adult corals described as *sessile*?

16. Explain asexual reproduction in coral.

17. How do coral reproduce sexually?

18. Why are coral reefs considered valuable ecosystems?

19. What happened to coral reefs during the 1997 to 1998 El Niño season?

20. List some threats to corals reefs caused by humans.

21. Name at least four sources of pollution that damage coral reefs.

22. Why are coral diseases occurring more frequently than in the past?

23. Why should coral reefs be protected?

What's Going On?

Coral reefs, some of the most productive places on Earth, are critically important marine ecosystems. One-fourth of all marine species and half of the fish caught commercially live on or around reefs. Reefs are also valuable resources for humans. Because coral reefs support so many different kinds of organisms, they are natural places for scientists to search for new drugs. Hundreds of medications, including the drug *AZT* which is used to treat *HIV*, have been derived from organisms on the reefs. In addition, reefs are natural barriers against incoming waves that protect the coast from damage during storms. Tourism in regions adjacent to reefs generates incomes for thousands of individuals.

Reefs are damaged by natural storms and fluctuations in weather, but their most serious threats are *anthropogenic*, related to humans. A list of specific and widely spread threats has been compiled by the Coral Reef Task Force. The top seven problems are the following:

1. Pollution, including sediments and chemicals that drain into the water from nearby landmasses

2. Overfishing, both commercially and for recreation

3. Destructive fishing practices, such as using cyanide or dynamite to kill or stun catches

4. Dredging and changes to the shoreline, primarily to ease the movement of ships

5. Grounding of ships and damage caused by ship anchors

6. Outbreaks of coral diseases

7. Changes in global climate that have unnaturally increased ocean temperature, frequency of storms, and rises in ocean levels

Connections

Coral reefs are primarily found in tropical oceans where waters are clear and temperatures and pH are ideal. Most of the U.S. coral reefs are in the western Pacific (Hawaii, Guam, American Samoa, and Commonwealth of Northern Mariana Islands). The remainder are off the coasts of Florida, Texas, Puerto Rica, and the U.S. Virgin Islands. These reefs are shown as orange dots in the map in Figure 2. Like reefs around the world, U.S. coral reefs are in danger because they are very sensitive to changes in the environment.

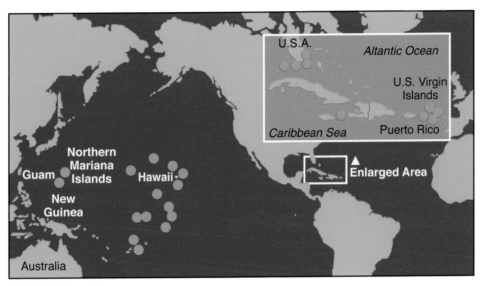

● = coral reef

Figure 2

U.S. coral reefs

One of the biggest threats to coral reefs is related to global climate change. Levels of carbon dioxide in the air are at an all-time high due to combustion of fossil fuels for production of electricity and to power vehicles. At the interface of air and ocean, some of this carbon dioxide dissolves in the water, increasing its acidity. Corals are not able to build their skeletons when ocean water is acidic. Carbon dioxide in air also increases the thickness of the greenhouse gases, causing Earth's surface temperature to rise. If temperatures exceed 84.2°F (29°C), corals expel the algae that live with them. The solution to both problems sounds simple: reduce the output of carbon dioxide. However ways to implement this solution are difficult to find. The situation is serious, but well worth pursuing. With a little help, damaged reefs can survive and bounce back.

Want to Know More?

See appendix for Our Findings.

Further Reading

Levin, Ted. "To Save a Reef," National Wildlife Federation. Available online. URL: http://www.nwf.org/nationalwildlife/article. cfm?issueid=22&articleid=687. Accessed July 17, 2008. Levin describes the condition of the reefs off the coast of Florida.

Silvera, Janet. "Coral Catastrophe—At Least 845 Reef Species Hit Red List," *The Gleaner*, Jamaica, W.I. July 15, 2008. Available online. URL: http://www.jamaica-gleaner.com/gleaner/20080715/life/life2.html. Accessed July 17, 2008. Silvera reports on the latest findings of the International Coral Reef Symposium.

Tacio, Henrylito. "Coral Bleaching Once More Centre Stage," People and Planet, July 15, 2008. Available online. URL: http://www.peopleandplanet. net/doc.php?id=3337. Accessed July 17, 2008. Tacio explains how global warming contributes to coral bleaching.

3. Carbon Footprint

Topic

A carbon footprint reflects the impact of a person's activities on the environment.

Introduction

Our planet owes its comfortably warm temperatures to *greenhouse gases*. Solar radiation travels through the atmosphere, strikes Earth's surface, and is changed to heat (see Figure 1). Some of the heat is released into space, but much is trapped near the Earth by the dome of greenhouse gases. Without these gases, Earth's surface would be very cold.

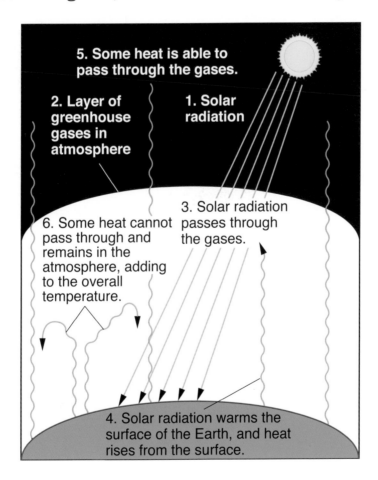

Figure 1

Levels of greenhouse gases are increasing rapidly, causing Earth's surface temperature to rise. *Global warming* is an overall increase in the Earth's temperature due to a thickening of the greenhouse gases in the atmosphere. The two primary greenhouse gases are carbon dioxide and methane.

Carbon dioxide is released into the atmosphere by combustion of fossil fuels. The principal sources of carbon dioxide emissions are power plants and transportation. As a result, many of our daily activities create carbon dioxide emissions. Every time you plug in an appliance or flip on a light, you are increasing levels of greenhouse gases. The same thing happens when you ride in a car, bus, or plane. In this activity, you will learn more about your *carbon footprint,* which shows how much you contribute to greenhouse gases.

Time Required

55 minutes

Materials

- access to the Internet
- science notebook

Safety Note　　Please review and follow the safety guidelines at the beginning of this volume.

Procedure

1. To learn more about a carbon footprint, go to the Web site http://www.thenatureconservancy.com/initiatives/climatechange/calculator/?src=f1. This site is provided by The Nature Conservancy, a nonprofit environmental organization, that can help you determine how much carbon dioxide your activities contribute to the atmosphere.

2. Read the information under "Get Started" and select the number that tells how many individuals live in your home. Then select "Calculated for My Household."

3. Under "Home Energy," indicate the type and number of bedrooms in your home. Select the state in which you live. Answer the questions under "What Have You Done to Change Your Impact?" Then click "Continue."

4. Under "Driving and Flying," answer the questions related to your family's travel habits. Click "Continue."

5. Under "Food and Diet," answer the questions related to your family's eating habits. Click "Continue."

6. Under "Recycling and Waste," answer the questions related to your family's habits. Click "Continue." Record you carbon footprint in your science notebook.

7. Read the tab titled "Climate Saving Tips" on the left side of the page.

8. Repeat the calculation procedure again. This time, indicate that your family:

    a. does not fly

    b. drives only 5,000 miles (mi) (8,047 kilometers [km]) each year

    c. uses Energy Star appliances

    d. has done everything possible to conserve energy

    e. eats organic food

9. Answer Analysis questions 1 through 8.

10. To learn about compact fluorescent light (CFL) bulbs, go to the HowStuffWorks Web page: http://home.howstuffworks.com/question236.htm. Read the information on this site.

11. Answer Analysis questions 9 and 10 in your science notebook.

12. To learn more about energy efficient light bulbs, go to http://www.energystar.gov/index.cfm?c=cfls.pr_cfls. This Web site is provided by the Environmental Protection Agency (EPA). Read the paragraph on CFL bulbs.

13. Answer Analysis questions 11 and 12 in your science notebook.

Analysis

1. What is your family's carbon footprint?

2. How did the carbon footprint change after step 8?

3. Some companies offer the opportunity to offset one's carbon footprints. If individuals make a donation, the companies will use

the money to help offset your use of electricity. What are some of the ways the Nature Conservancy helps offset carbon footprints?

4. Describe some of the ways Patrick Gonzalez, who was discussed under "Climate-Saving Tips," reduced his contributions to the greenhouse effect.

5. List five things you and your household could do to reduce global warming.

6. How can planting more trees reduce your carbon footprint?

7. Explain in your own words what the phrase, "think globally, act locally," means.

8. What is The Nature Conservancy? What has it accomplished since its inception?

9. What is a CFL bulb?

10. Why does an incandescent bulb get hot while a CFL bulb remains relatively cool?

11. How much electricity could we save if everyone replaced one incandescent bulb with a CFL bulb?

12. How much energy does a CFL bulb save compared to an incandescent bulb?

What's Going On?

Although levels of greenhouse gases were relatively stable for thousands of years, they have been increasing since 1750. During the era of the *Industrial Revolution*, which occurred in the mid–1800s, the atmosphere experienced a sharp increase in carbon dioxide levels (see Figure 2). Studies have shown that as levels of carbon dioxide have increased, so has Earth's surface temperature.

The problems caused by increasing carbon dioxide and rising temperatures are global. However, the actions of each individual can make a difference. Everyday choices can help in two ways: they can reduce greenhouse gases and increase the uptake of carbon dioxide. Each person can adjust his or her lifestyle to cut back on activities that produce greenhouse gases. Selecting locally grown food, resetting the thermostat to use less electricity, and using public transportation are good options that help the environment.

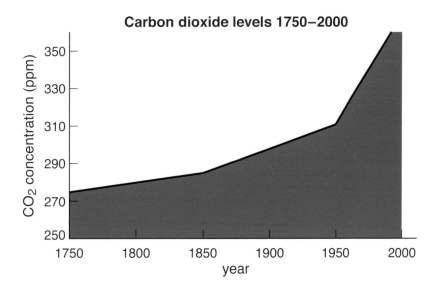

Figure 2

Connections

Scientists know that the Earth's surface is getting warmer because of studies they have done on ancient ice. At the poles, new snow and ice are laid down annually on top of earlier years', creating layers. By taking *ice cores* (see Figure 3), scientists can analyze ice that is thousands of years old. Bubbles of gas trapped in each layer tell us what, and how much, gases were present.

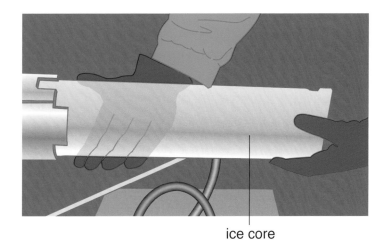

ice core

Figure 3

Analysis of ice cores confirms that Earth's surface temperature is gradually getting warmer and levels of carbon dioxide and methane are rising. Since the Industrial Revolution, carbon dioxide levels have increased by 3.3 percent. Methane levels show a similar increase.

The Intergovernmental Panel on Climate Change (IPCC) predicts that at the current rate of warming, the Earth's surface temperature will increase enough by 2100 to cause sea levels to rise as much as 3 feet (ft) (0.9 meters [m]). The IPCC provides information on each country's contributions to global warming. Industrialized countries like the United States and European nations are the biggest offenders. Citizens of these well-developed societies are responsible for working together and taking the lead toward a global solution.

Want to Know More?

See appendix for Our Findings.

Further Reading

ScienceDaily. "Ice Cores Reveal Fluctuations in Earth's Greenhouse Gases," May 17, 2008. Available online. URL: http://www.sciencedaily.com/releases/2008/05/080514131131.htm. Accessed July 8, 2008. This Web page explains the natural fluctuations in temperature and correlates them to levels of greenhouse gases.

Sierra Club. "Global Warming," 2008. Available online. URL: http://www.sierraclub.org/globalwarming/dangerousexperiment/solutions.asp. Accessed July 18, 2008. The Sierra Club is a century-old organization dedicated to conservation. This page on its Web site provides information on the causes and effects of global warming.

Union of Concerned Scientists. "Global Warming," 2009. Available online. URL: http://www.ucsusa.org/global_warming/. Accessed February 7, 2009. This Web page offers links to sites with suggestions for reducing greenhouse emissions.

4. Virtual Fetal Pig Dissection

Topic

A virtual dissection reveals the gross anatomy of a fetal pig.

Introduction

Fetal pigs are excellent specimens for anatomical study because they have many structures in common with humans. Pigs are *mammals*, warm-blooded animals that maintain their body temperature, are covered with hair, and feed their young from *mammary glands*. Pigs, like humans, develop in a *placenta*. The unborn pigs are attached to the placenta with *umbilical cords*.

Most of the anatomical structures in pigs and humans are analogous. The differences are primarily due to the structural distinctions between two-and four-legged animals. In addition, the human liver has four lobes while the pig liver has five. Unlike humans, the first part of the large intestine in the pig is coiled. At the point of attachment of the small and large intestines, pigs have a *cecum*, a blind pouch that helps in digestion. Humans have a remnant of the cecum, the appendix. In female pigs, the uterus is *bicornate*, meaning that it has two cavities instead of one central cavity as in humans.

Although most of the blood vessels in the thoracic cavity are the same, there are a few differences. In fetal pigs, the brachiocephalic artery divides into the right subclavian and the bicarotid trunk, which subdivides into the left and right carotid arteries (see Figure 1). Humans lack a bicarotid trunk; the left carotid comes directly from the aorta, while the right carotid branches off the brachiocephalic artery. Most other structures in the abdominal and thoracic cavities are the same.

In this experiment, you will examine the external and internal structures of a preserved fetal pig through a virtual dissection. Figure 2 shows the fetal pig and some of its external structures.

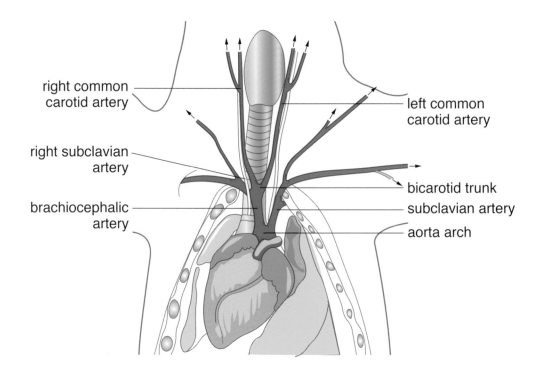

Figure 1

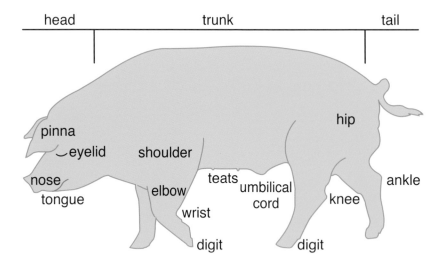

Figure 2

Time Required

55 minutes

Materials

⟜ computer

⟜ access to the Internet

⟜ science notebook

Safety Note   Please review and follow the safety guidelines at the beginning of this volume.

Procedure

1. Go to the Web site http://www.whitman.edu/biology/vpd/.

2. Click on "Virtual Fetal Pig Dissection."

3. Under "Study Guides," select "Anatomical References."

4. Select each of the five tabs, one at a time, and review the information provided. Answer Analysis questions 1 through 4.

5. In your science notebook, draw a picture of a fetal pig and label these regions:

    a. anterior

    b. posterior

    c. dorsal

    d. ventral

6. On the same drawing, show the saggittal, transverse, and frontal planes.

7. Under "Study Guides," select "Sexing Your Pig." Answer Analysis questions 5 and 6.

8. Under "Study Guides," select "Digestive System." Answer Analysis questions 7 through 25.

9. Under "Study Guides," select "Excretory System." Answer Analysis questions 26 through 30.

10. Under "Study Guides," select "Circulatory System." Answer Analysis questions 31 through 40.

11. Under "Study Guides," select "Reproductive System." Answer Analysis questions 41 and 42.

12. Under "Study Guides," select "Respiratory System." Answer Analysis question 43.

13. Under "Study Guides," select "Nervous System." Answer Analysis questions 44 through 46.

14. Complete each of the "Quizzes" on the Web site.

Analysis

1. The cranial region is (anterior/posterior) to the pectoral region.

2. In a (sagittal/transverse/frontal) section, an imaginary plane is passed through the pig separating it into equal left and right halves.

3. The fetal pig's spine is (medial/lateral) to its shoulders.

4. Using the spine as a point of reference, the fetal pig's toes are (proximal/distal) to its foreleg.

5. How can you distinguish a male and female pig?

6. Where does the urogenital tract open in a male pig?

7. What is the function of the paired nares?

8. Taste buds in the _____ are located along the tongue. Describe the appearance of the tongue.

9. Describe the location of one of the salivary glands.

10. Describe the differences in the hard and soft palates.

11. What are unerupted teeth?

12. The _____ is the junction of the passageway of the _____ (along which food travels to the stomach) and the _____ (along which air travels to the lungs).

13. When the pig swallows, the _____ prevents food from entering the lungs.

14. What is the large, dark brown structure in the upper quadrant of the pig's abdomen?

15. How can you locate the stomach?

16. What is the approximate length of the small intestine?

17. What is the function of the small intestine?

18. How does the large intestine differ in appearance from the small intestine?

19. Where is the gallbladder? What is its function?

20. What is the function of the pyloric sphincter?

21. What are rugae in the stomach?

22. Where is the spleen in relation to the stomach?

23. What is the function of the rectum?

24. What is the function of the pancreas?

25. What are the functions of the mesenteries?

26. What is the function of the excretory system?

27. Where are the kidneys located?

28. What are the functions of the kidneys?

29. Unfiltered blood enters the kidneys through _____. Filtered blood leaves the kidneys through _____.

30. Urine travels from the kidneys through _____ to the bladder. The _____ is a tube that carries urine from the bladder to the exterior.

31. What membranous structure covers the heart?

32. What two organs are adjacent to the heart?

33. Where is the thymus gland located? What is its function?

34. Where is the coronary artery? What is its function?

35. How do the atria differ from the ventricles in color and size?

36. Describe the path of the aorta as it leaves the heart.

37. In an adult pig, which ventricle is thicker, the left or right? Why?

38. Which chamber of the heart receives deoxygenated blood from the body?

39. Which chamber receives oxygen rich blood from the lungs?

40. Where are heart valves located? What is their function?

41. Describe the position and appearance of ovaries, oviducts, and uterus in the female pig.

42. Describe the position and appearance of the testicles and epididymae of the male pig.

43. Describe the path of air from the nares to the lungs.

44. What membranes cover the brain?

45. Name three structures that can be seen on the ventral surface of the brain.

46. Where is the thalamus? What is its function?

What's Going On?

Virtual dissections have many advantages. These exercises provide excellent experiences for those who do not want to participate in actual dissections. Alternately, a virtual dissection can be used to preview work that will be done during an actual dissection.

Dissection, the process of taking apart and observing a once-living thing to see how it works, is valued in the study of anatomical structures. Both actual and virtual dissections help connect the abstract concepts of biology and anatomy to real structures. Pigs are especially useful because their organ systems are very similar to those of humans. As a result, they are the animals of choice in most human anatomy classes. Pigs are also important dissection specimens in comparative anatomy classes in which students compare the structures of different animals including fish, sharks, amphibians, and reptiles.

Fetal pigs used in virtual and actual dissections are a by-product of the meat industry. When pregnant sows are slaughtered for food, their developing fetuses are removed and saved for classroom study. The fetal pigs are prepared by injection with preserving fluid. In addition, preparation may include injection of colored latex into the circulatory system. Red latex is used in the arterial system and blue in the venous system.

Connections

Dissection of humans is most often reserved for students studying medicine and graduate students in various fields of biomedical research. Human cadavers used in dissection come from individuals who donated their bodies to science. Bodies are prepared by removing the blood and replacing it with embalming fluid. The body is also immersed in embalming fluid for several months. The primary chemicals in embalming are formaldehyde and phenol. In high concentrations, these are *carcinogens*, so they are used in low concentrations to prepare the bodies. In many cases, the bodies are cremated after dissection, then the ashes returned to the families.

Want to Know More?

See appendix for Our Findings.

Further Reading

Animal Welfare Institute. "Breaking Old School Habits," Available online. URL: http://www.awionline.org/pubs/Quarterly/06-55-01/06_55_1p16. htm. Accessed July 11, 2008. On this Web site, the author points out several alternatives to animal dissection.

Correll, DeeDee. "For Human Dissection Needs, the Body Count Is Low," *Los Angeles Times*, May 26, 2008. Available online. URL: http://www. articles.latimes.com/2008/may/26/nation/na-cadavers26. Accessed July 11, 2008. Correll discusses the need for more bodies for use in graduate-level biomedical courses and in medical school.

Devlin, Ed. "Fetal Pig Dissection." Available online. URL: http://people. hsc.edu/faculty-staff/edevlin/edsweb01/new_page_14.htm. Accessed July 16, 2008. Ed Devlin's home page on the Hampden-Sydney College Web site offers an excellent review of fetal pig dissection, using diagrams to illustrate it.

5. Conservation of Mass

Topic

Early experiments related to mass helped lead to today's understanding of conservation of mass.

Introduction

A chemical reaction occurs when two or more substances react and undergo chemical changes. During a chemical reaction, one or more new substances are formed.

Some chemical reactions happen so slowly that an observer cannot see a change occurring. For example, the formation of rust from iron and oxygen is a gradual chemical change. However, others are more obvious. If you light a sparkler (see Figure 1), the magnesium in it combusts and the sparkler gives off heat and light. Other indicators of chemical reactions include bubbling, sound, production of an odor, or a change in color.

Figure 1

A sparkler gives off heat and light.

In all chemical reactions, matter and energy undergo changes. In the sparkler reaction, matter was converted into heat and light energy. A chemical reaction that produces heat is described as *exothermic*. Other types of reactions take up energy, and these are described as *endothermic*. Reactants undergoing endothermic reactions feel cool to the touch. Photosynthesis is a endothermic reaction in which the a plant takes in the sun's energy to make glucose (Figure 2).

Some of the most important work on changes of matter and energy was done by Antoine-Laurent Lavoisier (1743–94), a young Frenchman who conducted experiments in his home with the help of his wife, Marie Anne (1758–1836). In this experiment, you are going to learn more about Lavoisier and his research.

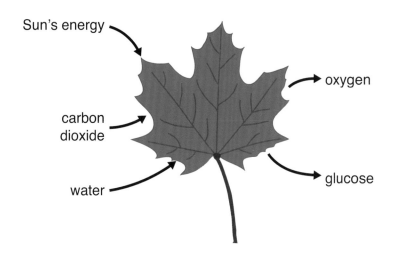

Figure 2

Photosynthesis

Time Required

30 minutes for Part A
30 minutes for Part B

Materials

- 1/2 teaspoon (tsp) baking soda
- 1/2 tsp citric acid

- 1 quart-size Ziploc™ freezer bag
- small beaker
- 40 milliliters (ml) water
- triple-beam balance or electronic scale
- access to the Internet
- science notebook

Safety Note Wear gloves and goggles when working with chemicals. Please review and follow the safety guidelines at the beginning of this volume.

Procedure, Part A

1. Access the Internet and carry out searches to learn more about Antoine-Laurent Lavoisier. Specifically, find answers the Analysis questions 1 through 8.

Procedure, Part B

1. Place 1/2 tsp baking soda and 1/2 tsp citric acid into the Ziploc™ bag.

2. Pour 40 ml water into the beaker.

3. Carefully set the beaker of water into the Ziploc™ bag. Do not spill the water.

4. Place the Ziploc™ bag and beaker of water on the triple-beam balance or electronic scale. Do not let the water spill.

5. In your science notebook, record the mass of the bag, dry chemicals, and beaker of water.

6. Remove the bag from the scale and seal it tightly. Tip the beaker of water so that it mixes with the dry chemicals. Continue to hold the bag in your hands and observe what happens. (While you are holding the bags, do not squeeze or knead it.)

7. When the chemical reaction stops, place the sealed bag on the scale. Record the mass of the bag and its contents in your science notebook.

8. Answer Analysis questions 9 through 15.

Analysis

1. When and where did Lavoisier live?

2. What was his job?

3. Explain the *phlogiston* theory.

4. What did Lavoisier think of the phlogiston theory?

5. What types of laboratory techniques did Lavoisier use?

6. What is the law of conservation of mass? How did Lavoisier's work help establish it?

7. What was the role of Marie Anne Lavoisier in Antoine's research?

8. What is a chemical reaction?

9. How do you know that a chemical reaction took place in Part B of the experiment?

10. Was the chemical reaction in the bag endothermic or exothermic?

11. Did the mass of the bag and its contents change between measurements?

12. According to the law of conservation of mass, the mass of materials in a closed system will remain constant, regardless of changes that take place within the system. Allowing for errors in massing that could have occurred during the experiment, did Part B demonstrate the law of conservation of matter? Explain your answer.

13. How does this experiment support Lavoisier's work?

14. Lavoisier was very careful when he weighed chemicals. Why was it important for you to carefully weigh the bag before and after Part B of the experiment?

What's Going On?

Chemistry as a science did not exist until the mid-1700s. Predecessors of chemists, the ancient *alchemists*, knew of only four elements: fire, water, earth, and air (see Figure 3). The earliest chemists focused their efforts on understanding burning, or *combustion,* which they considered to be the most important chemical reaction. These scientists understood that corrosion of metals and respiration in animals were also forms of combustion.

Figure 3

The four elements of alchemy: (a) earth, (b) air, (c) water, and (d) fire

Phlogiston was believed to be the inflammable substance that every flammable material contained. When a flammable material burned, scientists thought that phlogiston was given off. For example, the combustion of wood was believed to produce two products, ash (which was called calx) and phlogiston. In a similar reaction, iron was thought to undergo a reaction to become rust (another form of calx) and phlogiston.

Lavoisier found fault with the phlogiston theory. Through meticulous quantitative measurements, Lavoisier demonstrated that when a metal burned, its weight increased because air was absorbed. He also showed that combustion of calx (wood ash) with charcoal gave off air. Lavoisier's work showed that phlogiston did not exist and that the total mass of matter does not change in a chemical reaction.

Connections

Lavoisier's interest in science was not limited to demonstrating that matter is conserved in chemical reactions. He also developed a method of naming compounds that is still in use today. He dismissed the old four-element way of looking at things and defined an element as anything that cannot be broken down into simpler elements. Lavoisier also found that air is a mixture of several gases and that water is made of two components, oxygen and hydrogen. Because Lavoisier did a lot of quantitative work, very carefully measuring reactants and products, he is recognized as a founder of *stoichiometry,* the field of science that quantifies the materials in a chemical reaction.

Despite his intense interests in chemistry, Lavoisier never pursued chemistry as a career. He was formally trained in law and intensely interested in French politics. Most of his adult life, Lavoisier worked as a tax collector. As a government employee, Lavoisier was very active is pushing for improvements that he felt were important. He supported the adoption of the metric system of uniform units of measurements. He also tried to introduce reforms to help the peasants whom he considered to be unfairly taxed. Some of Lavoisier's opinions lead to false accusations that he was a traitor to the government and he was beheaded. Less than two years after his death, his named was cleared and apologies for his execution were extended to his wife.

Want to Know More?

See appendix for Our Findings.

Further Reading

Chemical Heritage Foundation. "Antoine Laurent-Lavoisier," 2005. Available online. URL: http://www.chemheritage.org/classroom/ chemach/forerunners/lavoisier.html. Accessed July 13, 2008. This Web site provides descriptions of Lavoisier's achievements as well as a picture of his lab.

Giunta, Carmen. "Classic Chemistry," LeMoyne College, Department of Chemistry. Available online. URL: http://web.lemoyne.edu/~GIUNTA/ index.html. Accessed July 13, 2008. Giunta provides excellent discussions of the lives and work of many scientists, including Lavoisier.

Larson, Phillip Gardner. "Antoine Laurent Lavoisier." Available online. URL: http://cti.itc.virginia.edu/~meg3c/classes/tcc313/200Rprojs/lavoisier2/ home.html. Accessed July 13, 2008. This Web site provides of good overview of Lavoisier's life and works.

6. Astronaut Trading Cards

Topic

Astronauts have contributed to the advancement of space travel and exploration.

Introduction

An *astronaut*, or "star sailor," is a person trained to travel in space. Astronauts include both men and women from 34 countries. More than 500 highly trained astronauts have traveled in space. In the United States, the National Aeronautics and Space Administration (NASA) supervises research in space and trains astronauts.

In the late 1950s, the earliest astronauts were selected from experienced jet pilots. Today specialists and scientists who are not pilots also travel in space. On a space shuttle the four crew positions are commander, pilot, mission specialist, and payload specialist. The commander is responsible for the crew, flight safety, and the vehicle. The job of pilot is to help the commander operate the vehicle. Mission specialists carry out the shuttle's many jobs. Individuals who have specialized duties, but are not NASA-trained astronauts, are known as payload specialists. There may be several mission or payload specialists onboard a flight.

Because space flight is a relatively young branch of science, it has seen many firsts. The first living thing in space was not a human but a chimp named Ham. In January 1961, Ham made a 16-minute flight into space in a Project Mercury capsule. In April 1961, Yuri Gagarin (1934–68) of the Soviet Union was the first human in space. A month later, NASA sent Alan Shepherd (1923–98) on a 15-minute, suborbital flight on the *Freedom 7*. Almost a year later, John Glenn (1921–) piloted the *Friendship 7* on a three-orbit trip around the Earth. The first astronauts to walk on the Moon were Neil Armstrong (1930–) and Buzz Aldrin (1930–) in 1969, only 8 years after the first man in space (see Figure 1). In this experiment, you are going to select two astronauts that interest you, research their contributions to space travel, and share your findings with the class.

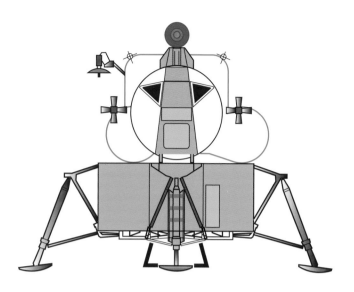

Figure 1

Moon-landing module

Time Required

55 minutes part A
30 minutes part B

Materials

- 2 index cards
- colored pencils or markers
- glue
- scissors
- access to the Internet
- printer
- science notebook

Safety Note   Please review and follow the safety guidelines at the beginning of this volume.

Procedure, Part A

1. Use the Internet to visit http://www.jsc.nasa.gov/Bios/more.html. This Web site lists the names and accomplishments of astronauts. Almost 500 astronauts have traveled in space.

2. Select two astronauts that interest you and write their names on the classroom board. Do not select names that other students have already chosen.

3. Conduct Internet research on the names you have selected. Find the following information about each astronaut:

    a. birth and death dates (if applicable)

    b. home

    c. education

    d. missions flown

    e. role on those missions

    f. age when flying mission(s)

    g. other interesting information

    h. picture

4. Write the information you find (a through g) in your science notebook.

5. Print a small picture of the astronaut. The picture should fit on an index card.

6. Use the picture and the information you gathered to create two astronaut trading cards. Your finished cards should contain all of the required information and be neat, attractive, and colorful.

Procedure, Part B

1. Swap your two trading cards with a classmate. Examine their cards and write down information about their astronauts in your science notebook.

2. Continue swapping cards until you have gathered information about 10 astronauts.

Analysis

1. What is an astronaut?

2. Why do you think the first "astronaut" was a chimp instead of a human?

3. Match the astronaut with the mission.

_____first U.S. astronaut in space

_____first astronaut to orbit the Earth three times

_____first person in space

_____one of the first men to walk on the Moon

a. John Glenn

b. Neil Armstrong

c. Alan Sheperd

d. Yuri Gagarin

4. List some of the jobs that astronauts are asked to do during space travel.

5. From your research and from reading other students' trading cards, what is the average age of an astronaut?

What's Going On?

New astronauts are selected every two years. Applicants for the job must have degrees in some area of math or science. Physically, applicants are required to have 20/20 eyesight (naturally or when they are wearing contact lenses or glasses), blood pressure below 140/90, and height from 62 to 75 inches (in.) (157.5 to 190.5 centimeters [cm]). Training is difficult and takes two or three years.

Today's astronauts are training for work on the International Space Station (ISS), an outpost developed by agencies from the United States, Russia, Japan, Canada, Europe, and Brazil. They receive instructions on all parts of the vehicle, including how to assemble it and how to carry out operations while in orbit. Astronauts must be able to work outside the station in extravehicular activities, conduct experiments, carry out maintenance, and use robotic equipment.

Missions on the ISS will last 3 to 6 months. Until 2010, astronauts will reach the ISS on board the shuttle. After that time, the shuttle will be retired and astronauts will travel to the station on the Russian Soyuz vehicle. For this reason, trainees must also be proficient with the Soyuz systems and operation.

Connections

NASA was established by President Dwight D. Eisenhower (1890–1969) in 1958 in response to the Soviet Union's 1957 launch of an unmanned satellite, *Sputnik.* In 1959, seven men were selected to train for Project Mercury, a mission to send a manned space craft in orbit. In 1961, President John F. Kennedy (1917–63) gave a boost to the space program by setting the goal of putting a man on the Moon and returning him safely to Earth before the end of the decade. Although this seemed like an almost insurmountable task, the Apollo 11 astronauts met the president's dream in 1969 when they landed on the Moon. Eventually, 12 astronauts walked on Moon.

After the Moon missions, NASA developed the space shuttle, a ship that could be used more than once. The first shuttle (see Figure 2) was launched in 1981. The Mars *Pathfinder* left Earth in 1997 to explore our closest planetary neighbor. In 2000, the International Space Station, a multinational project was put into place. From this outpost, scientists hope to learn more about space and space travel to benefit life on Earth.

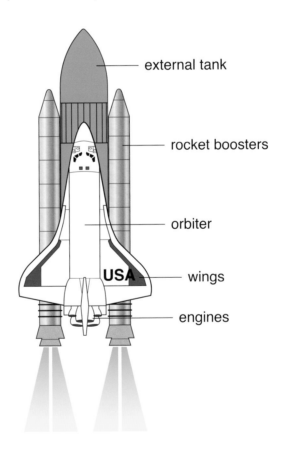

Figure 2

Want to Know More?

See appendix for Our Findings.

Further Reading

Cortright, Edgar M. "Apollo Expeditions to the Moon," February 13, 2006. Available online. URL: http://www.hq.nasa.gov/office/pao/History/SP-350/cover.html. Accessed July 18, 2008. Cortright gives a comprehensive history of the Apollo missions.

European Space Agency, Human Spaceflight and Exploration. "The International Space Station, a Test-bed for Future Space Exploration," July 17, 2008. Available online. URL: http://www.esa.int/esaHS/SEMZLGWIPIF_index_0.html. Accessed July 18, 2008. This Web page explains the jobs of astronauts on the International Space Station.

Lunar and Planetary Institute. "Exploring the Moon," 2008. Available online. URL: http://www.lpi.usra.edu/expmoon/. Accessed July 18, 2008. Information on the Moon and missions to the Moon are provided on this site.

7. Simple Machines

Topic

Simple machines make tasks easier to perform and are part of our daily lives.

Introduction

Almost every task we perform involves one or more of the six *simple machines*: lever, pulley, screw, inclined plane, wedge, and wheel and axle. Simple machines are useful because they either redirect or multiply the force needed to perform a task. The amount of *work* accomplished is not reduced by a simple machine. It is impossible to get more *energy* or work out of a system than is put into it. In fact, energy is lost in a simple machine in the form of *friction*. Nevertheless, the work feels easier and can generally be performed faster when a simple machine is used.

Since the amount of energy one puts into a system is the same as the energy one gets out, the following equation is true:

work in = work out

Work (*W*) is defined as a force (*F*) multiplied by a distance (*d*), so the equation can also be written as:

$$F_E d_E = F_R d_R$$

The subscript *E* stands for "effort" and represents what you put into the system, your input force. The subscript *R* represents what you get out of the system, the output force. Force is measured in *newtons* (N) and distance in meters (m).

An example illustrates how this formula is used. You might want to load a refrigerator into the back of a truck. There are basically two ways to do so: lift the refrigerator straight up or push the refrigerator up a ramp. The ramp obviously makes loading the refrigerator easier. However, since work in equals work out, you are performing the same amount of work in both cases. What is the difference? Using the ramp, the refrigerator travels a longer distance but requires less force.

How much faster and easier you can perform work represents a machine's *mechanical advantage (MA)*. Mechanical advantage can be defined as the

38

factor by which a machine multiplies effort force. A device that has a MA of 4 multiplies your effort force by 4. However, the cost for this increased effort force is increased distance. This same machine will require you to move the force 4 times farther.

The MA can be summarized as the ratio of resistance force to effort force. You can calculate MA two ways: by dividing resistance force by effort force or by dividing resistance distance by effort distance.

$$MA = \frac{F_R}{F_E} \qquad MA = \frac{d_R}{d_E}$$

In this experiment, you will review the principles of simple machines.

Time Required

55 minutes

Materials

- access to the Internet
- construction paper
- scissors
- colored pencils or markers
- pen or pencil
- science notebook

Safety Note   Please review and follow the safety guidelines at the beginning of this volume.

Procedure

1. Fold the piece of construction paper to make six flaps. To do so, examine Figure 1 as you carry out the following steps:
   a. Fold the paper in half the short way (Figure 1a).
   b. Fold the paper in quarters the short way (Figure 1b).
   c. Fold the paper in thirds the long way (Figure 1c).

d. Unfold the paper. Cut along the folds that are indicated in red (Figure 1d).

e. Fold all the flaps in toward the center (Figure 1e).

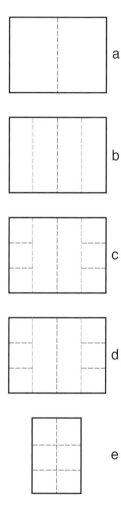

Figure 1

Folded construction paper

2. Access the Internet and search for Web sites that explain how simple machines work.

3. Using information you found in your research, draw and color a picture of one of the six simple machines on each flap. Write the name of the machine below the picture.

4. Inside the flap, use a pen or pencil to:

   a. Define the simple machine.

   b. Name six uses for the machine.

   c. Briefly explain how the machine makes work seem easier.

Analysis

1. What is the definition of *work*?

2. What are the units of force, distance, and work?

3. A simple machine cannot change the amount of work done. What does a simple machine change?

4. Since a simple machine cannot change the amount of work done, why do people use simple machines?

5. Based on your research, classify the six simple machines into either the lever group or the wedge group.

6. What is *mechanical advantage*?

7. Write and explain the formulas for mechanical advantage.

8. What is a lever?

9. How does a lever work?

10. Complete the label under each lever in Figure 2 to show if it is first, second, or third class. Then label the effort, load, and fulcrum on all three levers.

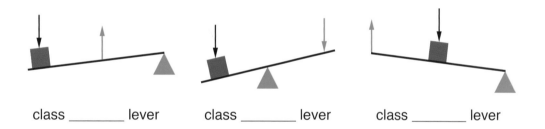

class _____ lever   class _____ lever   class _____ lever

Figure 2

Levers

11. Describe a pulley.

12. Does a pulley reduce the force required to move an object or change the direction in which the force moves?

13. Explain the difference between a fixed and a moveable pulley. Which one requires less effort on the part of the user?

14. What is a wheel and axle?

15. How does a wheel and axle work?

16. What is an inclined plane?

17. How does an inclined plane help you move objects?

18. Does the MA of an inclined plane increase or decrease as the slant decreases? Explain your answer.

19. How are a wedge and inclined plane different?

20. How is a screw similar to an inclined plane?

21. What is the pitch of a screw?

22. Calculate the MA in the following examples.

    a. Mark wants to lift a rock that weighs 600 N. He places a lever under the rock and pushes down with all his weight, 200 N. What is the MA of Mark's lever?

    b. Tasha wants to carry her travel trunk from the car to her dorm room. The trunk weighs 500 N and is too heavy to lift. Tasha rolls the trunk from her car into a wheelbarrow and easily transfers it to the dorm with 110 N of effort. What is the MA of the wheelbarrow?

    c. Somebody wants to lift a 2,000 N box with a pulley. The MA of his pulley is 10. How much force must somebody use to lift the whatever?

What's Going On?

Simple machines are all around us. First-class levers, which have the fulcrum between the effort and resistance force, include crowbars, scissors, pliers, tin snips, and playground seesaws. Wheelbarrows and bottle openers are two second-class levers. In these, the resistance is located between the fulcrum and the effort force. Sports use a lot of third-class levers, where the effort force is applied between the fulcrum and the resistance force. Tennis rackets, hockey sticks, baseball bats, fishing poles, and golf clubs are examples.

Pulleys may be fixed or moveable. A fixed pulley does not move; it eases work by changing the direction of a force. A moveable pulley rises up and down with the load, creating a mechanical advantage. Tow trucks and flag poles have pulleys. A wheel and axle is made of two wheels of different sizes that move together. Faucet handles, door knobs, wheels on cars and bicycles are wheels and axles. A ramp is one example of an inclined plane. Others include a slide or an escalator. Screws are inclined planes that are modified by wrapping the plane around a central axis. A wedge is also an inclined plane. Whereas an inclined plane remains stationary, a wedge moves. A knife, nail, and the front of a snow plow are examples of wedges.

Connections

Complex machines are made of many simple machines working together to make work easier. Cars, bicycles, and lawn mowers are complex machines made of combinations of simple machines. If you look at a bicycle, you can see some of the simple machines that make it up (see Figure 3). The frame of a bicycle is held together with screws. The wheels on a bike are actually wheels and axles. Petals are attached to levers that turn pulleys. Other levers on a bicycle are handlebars, handbrakes, and gear shifts. Together these make a complex machine that can do a lot of work with relative ease.

Figure 3

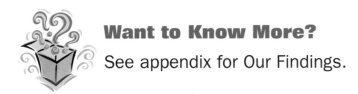

Want to Know More?

See appendix for Our Findings.

Further Reading

Explorelearning. "Levers." Available online. URL: http://www.explorelearning.com/index.cfm?method=cResource.dspView&ResourceID=646. Accessed October 23, 2008. This Web site includes a gizmo that demonstrates how levers work using a virtual lever.

Museum of Science. "Inventor's Toolbox," 1997. Available online. URL: http://www.mos.org/sln/Leonardo/InventorsToolbox.html. Accessed October 23, 2008. The elements of basic machines are explained on this Web site.

Utah State University Junior Engineering. "Simple Machine," October 7, 2003. Available online. URL: http://www.juniorengineering.usu.edu/workshops/machines/machines.php. Accessed October 23, 2008. Great explanations and drawings on the science of simple machines are provided on this Web site.

8. Hydrolysis and Dehydration Synthesis

Topic

Ball-and-stick models can demonstrate hydrolysis and dehydration synthesis in carbohydrates.

Introduction

Living things are made up of both *inorganic* and *organic compounds*. Generally, inorganic compounds are those that do not contain the element carbon. Water is the most important inorganic compound in organisms. Organic compounds are based on carbon, an element that is perfect for its central role in living things. Carbon has four electrons in its outer *valence shell*, giving it the ability to form four *covalent bonds*. These bonds can occur between carbon atoms or between carbon and other elements. For this reason, carbon easily forms long chains, as shown in Figure 1, as well as rings and other structures.

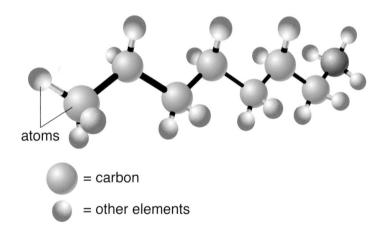

atoms

◯ = carbon

○ = other elements

Figure 1

Ball-and-stick model of carbon chain

There are four basic groups of organic compounds: carbohydrates, lipids, proteins, and nucleic acids. The first three are important parts of our diets. Carbohydrates include sugars and starches, which are made up of carbon, oxygen, and hydrogen. Carbohydrates are classified by size and solubility. The smallest carbohydrates are *monosaccharides* (mono means "one," saccharide denotes "sugar"). Monosaccharides are small enough to pass through a cell membrane, so they can travel from the blood into cells. *Glucose* is the most important monosaccharide in living things because cells can break down this simple sugar to make energy in the form of *ATP*. Others monosaccharides include fructose and galactose, which are different forms of glucose, as well as deoxyribose and ribose, sugars found in DNA and RNA respectively.

Two monosaccharides can join in the chemical reaction of *hydrolysis* to form a *disaccharide* ("two sugars"). Disaccharides include sucrose, which is also known as table sugar, and lactose, milk sugar. Disaccharides cannot pass through a cell membrane so they must be broken down into monosaccharides to be useful to the body. The breakdown of a disaccharide into two monosaccharides requires water and the process is called *hydrolysis*.

Several monosaccharides can form chains called polysaccharides ("many sugars"). Although monosaccharides dissolve easily in water, polysaccharides do not. Generally, the larger a carbohydrate molecule, the harder it is for that molecule to dissolve in water. This insolubility makes polysaccharides excellent storage molecules. Three important polysaccharides are *starch*, *glycogen,* and *cellulose*. Starch, a plant product, is found in foods like corn and potatoes. When we eat these foods, our bodies digest them and convert the carbohydrate molecules into glucose that our cells can use. Cellulose is also made by plants, but humans cannot digest it. Cellulose is important in the diet as fiber or bulk because it helps move digested foods through the intestines. Glycogen is a polysaccharide that stores glucose molecules in animal tissue. If blood levels of glucose get high, the body stores some as glycogen. If blood levels of glucose drop to low levels, the body breaks down some glycogen and circulates it in the blood. In this experiment, you will use models to show how glucose molecules participate in two chemical reactions, hydrolysis and dehydration synthesis.

Time Required

55 minutes for part A
55 minutes for part B

Materials

- ball-and-stick models (or gumdrops and toothpicks)
- colored pencils
- access to the Internet
- science notebook

Safety Note   Please review and follow the safety guidelines at the beginning of this volume.

Procedure, Part A

1. Access the Internet and carry out a search to find the ring structure of a glucose molecule. Draw the ring structure in your science notebook. Color the hydrogen atoms blue, the oxygen atoms red, and the carbon atoms green.

2. Search the Internet to find out what happens to glucose molecules when they undergo dehydration synthesis. Draw the process of two glucose molecules undergoing dehydration synthesis in your science notebook.

3. Continue your search to find what happens to a disaccharide when it undergoes hydrolysis. Draw the process of a disaccharide undergoing hydrolysis in your science notebook.

Procedure, Part B

1. Using ball-and-stick models (or gumdrops and toothpicks), create models of two glucose molecules. Refer to the drawings in your science notebook. Use blue balls (or gum drops) for hydrogen atoms, red balls (or gum drops) for oxygen atoms, and green balls (or gum drops) for carbon atoms.

2. Use your models of glucose molecules to show what happens when they undergo dehydration synthesis.

3. Use the model you created in step 2 to show what happens during hydrolysis.

Analysis

1. Explain the difference between organic and inorganic compounds.
2. Why is carbon able to form so many types of molecules?
3. Define *dehydration synthesis*.
4. Define *hydrolysis*.
5. During dehydration synthesis, one molecule of glucose loses an OH. What does the other molecule of glucose lose?
6. What do H and OH form?
7. During hydrolysis, two joined molecules of glucose are broken apart. In the process, one molecule of glucose gains an H. What does the other molecule of glucose gain?

What's Going On?

The ring structure of glucose is made of five carbon atoms and one oxygen atom joined to form a ring. The sixth carbon atom is attached to the carbon to the left of the oxygen atom (see Figure 2). Five hydroxyl groups (OH) are added to all of the carbon atoms except the one to the left of the oxygen, as shown in Figure 3. Seven hydrogen atoms are added at the positions shown in Figure 3.

When two glucose molecules join, the chemical reaction is called dehydration synthesis. This is an important process in making disaccharides and polysaccharides. During dehydration synthesis, the OH on one glucose molecule and H on another are removed, exposing the bonding sites of the two molecules (see Figure 4). The process gets its name from the fact that the two glucose molecules lose water (dehydration) to form a new molecule (synthesis).

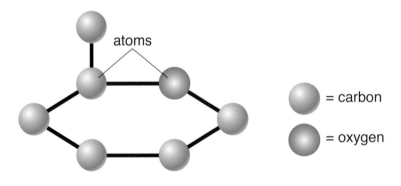

atoms

= carbon

= oxygen

Figure 2

Ball-and-stick model of glucose

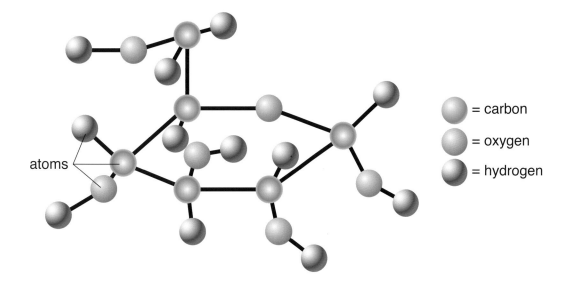

Figure 3

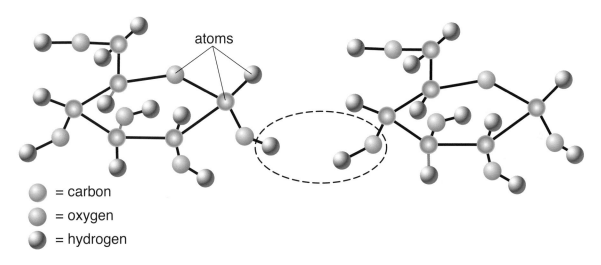

Figure 4

The reverse reaction occurs when the disaccharide breaks down into two glucose molecules. Hydrolysis (splitting with water) is the breakdown of a molecule by the addition of water. During hydrolysis of a disaccharide, hydrogen is added to one glucose molecule and hydroxide (OH) is added to the other to produce two complete molecules.

Connections

Carbohydrates are only one of the important organic compounds found in living things. The other three are proteins, lipids, and nucleic acids.

Proteins are long molecules made up of *amino acids*. There are 20 different amino acids, but they all have the same basic amine structure (NH_2) on one end and organic acid group (COOH) on the other. The differences among amino acids are due to their unique side groups, also known as the R group. When two amino acids join together, they do so by the process of dehydration synthesis. The bond between two amino acids is called a *peptide bond*. Like carbohydrates, they break apart by the process of hydrolysis.

Lipids are large molecules made of chains of fatty acids and glycerol molecules. They include fats and oils (triglycerides) that protect the body and store energy, phospholipids found in cell membranes, and steroids in cholesterol. Lipids do not dissolve in water, but will dissolve in organic solvents like ether and alcohol. The largest molecules in living things are nucleic acids, which are made up of carbon, hydrogen, oxygen, nitrogen, and phosphorus. Nucleic acids are made up of long chains of nucleotides. The two types of nucleic acids are DNA and RNA.

Want to Know More?

See appendix for Our Findings.

Further Reading

Brown, Terry. "Condensation and Hydrolysis," 1998. Available online. URL: http://www.tvdsb.on.ca/Westmin/science/sbioac/biochem/condense.htm. Accessed February 7, 2009. This Web site provide animations of condensation and hydrolysis and the role of enzymes.

"Dehydration Synthesis/Hydrolysis," April 17, 2008. Available online. URL: http://nhscience.lonestar.edu/biol/dehydrat/dehydrat.html. Accessed February 7, 2009. This interactive Web site shows animations of dehydration synthesis and hydrolysis.

Western Kentucky University. "Biochemistry." Available online. URL: http://bioweb.wku.edu/courses/biol115/Wyatt/Biochem/macromolecules.htm. Accessed October 23, 2008. This tutorial and animation walks through the steps of hydrolysis.

9. Using Cloud Patterns to Predict Weather

Topic

Local cloud patterns can be useful when making weather predictions.

Introduction

As you have probably been noticing since you were very young, clouds come in all shapes and sizes. Some look like animals, while others might remind you of clowns or monsters. However, you may not have realized that those different shapes can do more than just spark your imagination. The shape, altitude, and color of a cloud can tell a lot about the weather.

Clouds are classified into four basic types: *cumulus*, *stratus*, *cirrus*, and *nimbus*. The names of different types of clouds are based on Latin root words. *Cumulus* means "heap"; these are puffy clouds like the ones generally seen in fair weather. *Stratus* denotes "layer" and indicates clouds that appear in bands. The term *cirrus* signifies "curl," and the name describes thin, wispy clouds. Finally, *nimbus* means "rain." These clouds are dark, flat on the bottom, and known for producing precipitation. Clouds are classified further based on the height of the cloud base. Clouds found at the highest levels usually begin with *cirr-*, while those at middle levels begin with *alto-*. Different types of clouds are associated with different types of weather so the cloud patterns in the sky can be used to predict weather. In this experiment, you will observe different cloud patterns and use your observations to make weather predictions.

Time Required

45 minutes for part A
5 periods of 15 minutes each for part B

Materials

- access to the Internet
- access to an outdoor area
- science notebook

Safety Note	Please review and follow the safety guidelines at the beginning of this volume.

Procedure, Part A

1. Use the Internet to find pictures and information to complete Data Table 1 on cloud types.

Data Table 1			
Type of cloud	**Picture (sketch)**	**Description**	**Altitude**
Altocumulus			
Altostratus			
Cirrocumulus			
Cirrostratus			

Cirrus			
Cumulonimbus			
Cumulus			
Nimbostratus			
Stratocumulus			
Stratus			

Procedure, Part B

1.   Follow your teacher to an outdoor area. Observe the kinds of clouds that are in the sky. Be sure to notice the clouds that are low to the ground as well as those in the upper atmosphere. Record the types of clouds present and their relative abundance (none, scattered, numerous, dense) on Data Table 2.

2.   Make a prediction of the day's weather (temperature and chance of precipitation) based on your observations of cloud patterns.

3.   At the end of the day, check the weather online and make note of the temperature and chance or amount of precipitation on Data Table 2.

4.   Repeat steps 1 through 3 for four more days.

Data Table 2					
Day	Types of clouds	Abundance	Weather prediction	Actual weather (temperature and precipitation)	
1					
2					
3					
4					
5					

Analysis

1.   In your experiment, what type of clouds appeared on sunny, pleasant days? On days when it rained? On days prior to a rainy day?

2.   How did your predictions compare to the daily weather reports?

3.   Were you able to accurately predict weather patterns by observing the clouds? Explain why or why not.

4.   How were the type and abundance of clouds related to the temperature during the day?

5.   Other than observing the clouds in the sky, what are some other ways that you could predict weather patterns?

What's Going On?

High-altitude clouds (cirrostratus, cirrocumulus, and cirrus) are more useful for predicting weather on a long-term basis than clouds at lower altitudes. If the high-altitude cirrostratus or cirrocumulus are thick, there will typically be rain in the next two to three days. Rapidly moving high-altitude clouds means that bad weather will arrive quickly. Thin cirrus clouds generally indicate that fair weather is on the way.

Middle-altitude clouds can usually predict the weather conditions within a given day. Altostratus or altocumulus clouds tend to appear less than 24 hours before precipitation. If these mid-level clouds have a great deal of contrast between dark and light regions, there is a good chance of rain that day.

Low-level clouds generally indicate the current weather conditions in an area. Small, white, puffy cumulus clouds are known as fair-weather cumulus and are common when the weather is nice. However, these clouds can quickly turn into cumulonimbus clouds that can bring on a severe thunderstorm. Stratocumulus clouds are low and bumpy, and even though they may appear grey, they do not always bring rain. They can, however develop into rain clouds within a short period of time. Stratus clouds often bring snow or drizzle, and nimbostratus clouds are usually a sure sign of rain.

Connections

Clouds are made up of water vapor and ice crystals that result from the condensation of moisture in the atmosphere. The water vapor in clouds can evaporate just as quickly as it condensed to form the clouds, depending on the temperature and atmospheric pressure. Often, though, if a cloud becomes very large, the water or ice built up inside it falls to the ground as precipitation. The type of precipitation that falls depends mostly on the temperature in the atmosphere.

Even when it is warm on the surface of the Earth, the atmosphere can be cold enough to form ice crystals within clouds. However precipitation must pass through several "layers" of the atmosphere before it reaches the ground. When the entire atmosphere is warm, or there is warm air near the ground, precipitation generally falls as rain or drizzle. If the air is cold from the clouds to the ground, ice crystals melt slightly, enough to stick to each other and form snowflakes. If there is a warm layer of air within the atmosphere, but it is cold near the ground, ice crystals melt as they pass through the warm air, then freeze again into sleet as they get closer to the surface. When the atmosphere is warm at higher levels, but very cold on the ground, rain may fall and then freeze: this is known as freezing rain.

Cumulonimbus clouds (thunderheads) can form hailstones because of the strong updraft within the very tall and towering cloud. Ice crystals build up as the hailstones are pushed up and then fall down in a circular motion within the cloud. When the hailstones become too heavy to be contained in the cloud, they fall to Earth. Hail is generally so large that it falls as ice, regardless of the atmospheric temperature.

 ## Want to Know More?

See appendix for Our Findings.

Further Reading

Boatsafekids. "How to Be a Storm Spotter," 2007. Available online. URL: http://www.boatsafe.com/kids/weather1.htm. Accessed August 10, 2008. This Web site provides great photographs of different types of clouds.

Department of Atmospheric Sciences, University of Illinois. "Clouds and Precipitation." Available online. URL: http://ww2010.atmos.uiuc.edu/ (Gh)/guides/mtr/cld/home.rxml. Accessed August 14, 2008. Great photographs and descriptions of clouds are provided on this Web site.

Lorentz, Katie. "Scientists Studying Wintry Ice in Summer Clouds." NASA, January 28, 2005. Available online. URL: http://www.nasa.gov/centers/langley/science/ice_crystals.html. Accessed August 10, 2008. In this article, Lorentz describes work by NASA's Langley Research Center in Hampton, Virginia, on ice crystal found in summer storm clouds in Florida.

10. Create a Climatogram

Topic

Local temperature and levels of precipitation can be used to create a climatogram.

Introduction

The weather conditions can change daily. You probably check the weather report every day before deciding what to wear or whether or not to bring an umbrella with you when you leave the house. Although the weather may vary from day to day in an area, the *climate* of an area is generally predictable. *Climate* is the average pattern of weather in a region over several years.

A *climatogram* is a combination of a line graph and a bar graph that shows the average temperature and precipitation in an area. In a yearly climatogram, the average monthly precipitation is plotted as a bar graph along the X-axis, and the average monthly temperature is plotted as a line graph (see Figure 1). Sometimes the average high and low temperatures are plotted separately on the chart. The information that is generally used to create a climatogram is compiled over 30 years or more. In this experiment, you will create a miniature climatogram by compiling and plotting the average precipitation and temperature in your area over a period of two weeks and compare it to an actual climatogram for the area.

Time Required

45 minutes on day 1
10 minutes per day for the next 13 days

Materials

- ◆ access to the Internet
- ◆ graph paper
- ◆ ruler

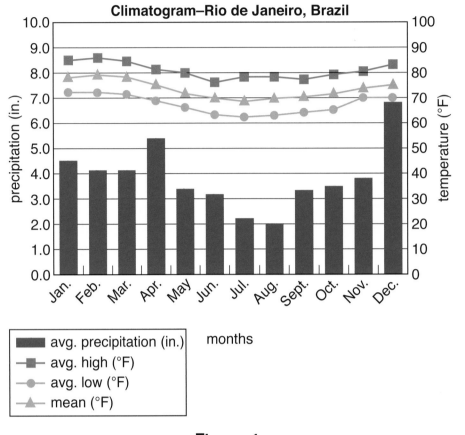

Figure 1

Sample climatogram

- ➡ colored pencils or markers
- ➡ science notebook

Safety Note Please review and follow the safety guidelines at the beginning of this volume.

Procedure

1. Access a local yearly weather chart online to find temperature and precipitation for each month (including this month) within the past year in your region (state, county, city, or section of the United States). Use the information to create a yearly climatogram. To do so:

   a. Create a graph with each of the 12 months listed along the X-axis, precipitation along the Y-axis on the right side, and temperature along the Y-axis on the left side.

   b. Mark the Y-axis so that every 1 inch (in.) of precipitation lines up with every 10 degrees in Fahrenheit (°F) temperature.

   c. Use the information from the weather chart to create the bars on the bar graph and points on the line graph.

2. Access the daily weather reports online each day for 14 days. Write the reports in your science notebook.

3. Record the daily average temperature and amount of rainfall for your city on the data table.

4. Create a graph with each of the 14 days listed along the X-axis, precipitation along the Y-axis on the right side, and temperature along the Y-axis on the left side. Mark the Y-axes so that every 1 in. of precipitation lines up with every 10°F.

Data Table														
Day	1	2	3	4	5	6	7	8	9	10	11	12	13	14
Avg. Temp.														
Precip.														

Analysis

1. Examine the climatogram you made in step 1. What was the average temperature and the precipitation for this month last year?

2. How do the temperature and amount of precipitation in your mini (14-day) climatogram compare to the average for this month in the yearly climatogram completed in step 1?

3. Research the climate in your area and locate a completed long-term climatogram for your region. How does this climatogram compare to the one created in step 1?

4. Explain why the climatogram created from one year of data may have been different from the long-term climatogram.

5. What factors can cause the weather conditions in an area to change from one day to the next? From one year to the next?

What's Going On?

Official climatograms are created using temperature and precipitation data from an area that is usually compiled for decades. The reason for this lengthy data compilation is to ensure that the figures on the graph are not distorted by years that fall above or below the norm. In any given year, the temperature and precipitation for an area can fluctuate significantly due to several factors including El Niño and La Niña events as well as global warming. Therefore, if some years have higher or lower averages than others, the fact that there are many years used to find the average compensates for any variation that occurs.

Climatograms represent the climate of an area. Latitude, altitude, terrain, snow or ice cover, ocean currents, and atmospheric conditions can all influence the climate of an area. Globally, climates are used to classify regions into *biomes*, which are areas that are similar in climate. Since biomes are generally in geographically similar areas and have similar climates, they tend to contain similar types of organisms. Therefore, biomes have characteristic species of plants and animals due to the specific type of climate in that region.

Connections

The climate in an area can change over a period of time due to many naturally occurring phenomena. Shifts in air and water currents such as *El Niño* and *La Niña* can create regular changes in weather patterns over large portions of the globe. Additionally, climate can be affected by the intensity of sunlight that warms the Earth. Solar intensity varies on an 11-year cycle and can also change on a long-term scale. Other natural phenomena such as volcanic eruptions can alter the climate in an area drastically for a period of several years.

In recent years, the climate around the world has changed due to human activity. Since the Industrial Revolution in the late 1800s, humans have relied on fossil fuels such as coal and petroleum products for industry and transportation. The burning of fossil fuels contributes to the amount of carbon dioxide and other greenhouse gases in the atmosphere. Greenhouse gases trap the heat from the Sun near the Earth's surface, increasing the temperature, a phenomenon known as *global warming*. Global warming has caused the average global climate to increase in temperature by several degrees in the past 100 years. Although this increase does not seem like a large amount, it can upset the delicate balance that exists in many ecosystems on Earth.

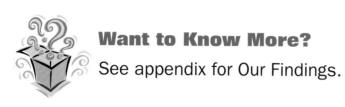

Want to Know More?

See appendix for Our Findings.

Further Reading

Earth Floor. "Biomes: How to Read a Climatogram," 2004. Available online. URL: http://www.cotf.edu/ete/modules/msese/earthsysflr/climograph.html. Accessed October 26, 2008. This Web site explains how to read a climatogram and the relationship between a climatogram and a biome.

Globe Learning Program. "Match the Biome Game." Available online. URL: http://www.globe.gov/fsl/events/helsinki2/templ.cgi?biome_match&lang=en&nav=1. Accessed October 26, 2008. Globe Learning has created a fun and informative game that shows how to use a climatogram to understand the conditions of specific biomes.

Learning Exchange. "Chaparral: A Forgotten Habitat Resource Unit," 1998. Available online. URL: http://www.urbanedpartnership.org/target/units/chaparral/pages/climatograms.html. Accessed October 23, 2008. This Web site provides information on the chaparral biome, including climatic data that is displayed on a climatogram.

11. Mapping Lightning Strikes

Topic

The number of lightning strikes in regions can be analyzed graphically.

Introduction

Lightning is one of the most beautiful displays of weather phenomena in nature (see Figure 1). However, it is also one of the most dangerous weather occurrences known to man. Lightning is essentially an electrical discharge that occurs in the atmosphere, typically accompanying thunderstorms. During a storm, lightning can occur between two regions of a *cumulonimbus cloud* (thunderhead), between two completely different clouds, or between a cloud and the ground.

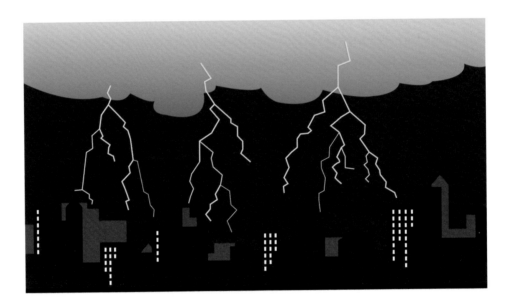

Figure 1

Lightning is an electrical discharge.

Scientists have documented and named several different types of lightning strikes, so they understand the basic physics behind these brilliant flashes of light. However, the true cause of lightning is still under debate in many scientific realms. Lightning occurs when there is a difference in electrical charge in the atmosphere, either between the upper and lower regions of a large thunderhead or between a cloud and the ground. This difference in charge produces an electrical release that travels at speeds exceeding 65,616 yards (yd) per second (60,000 meters [m] per second) at temperatures above 54,000 degrees Fahrenheit (°F) (30,000 degrees Celsius [°C]), The atmospheric and geological conditions in an area can influence the frequency of lightning strikes in a particular area. In this experiment, you will map lightning strikes in different states and create graphs comparing the frequency of lightning strikes in these different areas.

Time Required

30 minutes a day three days

Materials

- ◦◈ graph paper
- ◦◈ ruler
- ◦◈ colored pencils
- ◦◈ access to the Internet
- ◦◈ science notebook

Safety Note   Please review and follow the safety guidelines at the beginning of this volume.

Procedure

1. Select four states from the list provided by your teacher that you believe might experience a lot of lightning. Write the names of these states in your science notebook. Of these four, which state do you think will have the most lightning strikes? Write this state in Row 1 of the data table.

2. On the data table, write the state that you think will have the second highest number of lightning strikes in row 2, the state with the third highest number in row 3, and the state with the fewest lightning strikes in row 4.

3. Answer Analysis question 1.

4. Access the online lightning strike detector at intellicast.com at http://www.intellicast.com/Storm/Severe/Lightning.aspx. This Web site displays a U.S. map and indicates areas where lightning has struck in the last hour.

5. On the data table, make a note of the number of lightning strikes that have occurred in each of the states you listed. Record these strikes in the column titled "Lightning strikes on first observation."

6. Repeat steps 4 and 5 on two other occasions either at another time on the same day or on another day.

7. Under "Related Weather Maps," click on "Current Radar." Examine the four states you listed on the data table and see if the amount of rainfall shown by the current radar is related to the number of lightening strikes. Record your findings in your science notebook.

8. Under "Related Weather Maps," click on "Today's Forecast." Examine the four states you listed on the data table and see if the weather patterns shown are related to the number of lightning strikes. For example, is there a front moving into the area where lightening is occurring? Record your finding in your science notebook.

9. Answer Analysis questions 2 through 5.

Data Table			
States	Lightning strikes on first observation	Lightning strikes on second observation	Lightning strikes on third observation
1.			
2.			
3.			
4.			

Analysis

1. What factors do you think can increase lightning frequency in an area? Why do you think this is so?

2. Create a line graph plotting the lightning strikes for the four different states (each in a different color) during the three observation periods.

3. Which of the areas that you observed had the greatest lightning strike frequency? The least?

4. Does this information agree with what you expected to find? Why or why not?

5. Describe the weather conditions in the area receiving the most strikes.

What's Going On?

Lightning is formed when there is a difference in static electrical charges between two areas in the atmosphere. The reason for this charge difference is not known for certain, but many scientists believe it is due to the collision of ice particles rotating within the massive cumulonimbus clouds that develop during a thunderstorm. As ice particles collide, electrons are shed from the water molecules, causing a negatively charged region at the bottom of a cloud and a positively charged region at the top of the cloud (see Figure 2).

Often, the difference in charge will be released by a lightning strike within the cloud or even between two oppositely charged regions of separate clouds. However, on many occasions during a thunderstorm, the ground below the cloud becomes positively charged. Eventually, negative charges within the cloud are attracted to positive charges on the ground, forming a lightning strike that connects between the cloud and the ground. Some soil types, such as sand, are more likely to conduct electrical charges and therefore receive more cloud-to-ground lightning strikes than those containing other types of soil.

Connections

Thunderstorms are produced by cumulonimbus clouds, which occur when a front containing warm, moist air collides with a front containing cooler

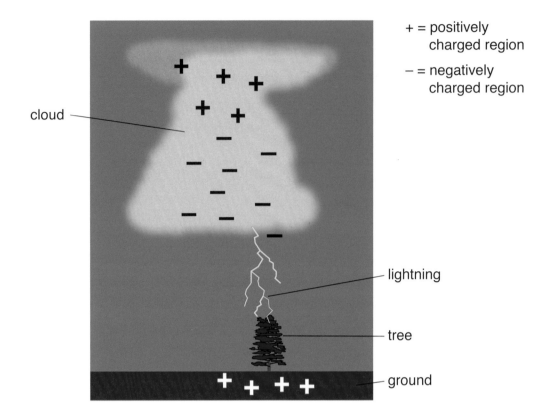

+ = positively
    charged region

− = negatively
    charged region

cloud

lightning

tree

ground

Figure 2

air. As the fronts run together, humidity that was contained in the warm air condenses, forming a very tall cloud. When the cloud accumulates too much condensed water to be contained, it releases rain. Sometimes, *hailstones* are produced along with the rain. Hailstones are accumulations of ice that are produced in cold regions within a cloud and circulating air currents. As the ice crystals rotate within the cloud, they grow larger as more ice crystallizes onto them, forming a hailstone.

The differences in temperature and the circulation of air and hail cause the cloud to accumulate charged particles in different regions. The discharge of electricity between positive and negative regions produces a lightning strike, which causes the air molecules to expand rapidly. This rapid expansion produces a sound wave, resulting in a loud noise known as thunder. The sound of thunder, as perceived by a listener, can range from a sharp, loud crack to long, low rumble. During a thunderstorm, lightning is seen before thunder is heard. This is because light travels faster than sound does. Therefore, if a storm is close to an observer, the observer will see the lightning and almost immediately hear thunder. When a storm is farther away, the lightning will be seen several seconds before the thunder is heard.

Want to Know More?

See appendix for Our Findings.

Further Reading

Astrogenic Systems. "Strikestar," 2008. Available online. URL: http://www.strikestarus.com/. Accessed September 1, 2008. This Web site shows lightning strikes all over the world.

National Geographic. "Lightning: The Shocking Story," 2008. Available online. URL: http://www.nationalgeographic.com/lightning/. Accessed September 1, 2008. This Web site, written for young people, explains the fundamentals of lightning and provides some great photographs.

Price, Steve, Patrick Barry, and Tony Phillips. "Where Lightning Strikes," NASA, December 5, 2001. Available online. URL: http://science.nasa.gov/headlines/y2001/ast05dec_1.htm. Accessed February 19, 2009. This Web site explains why lightning strikes in some places but not others.

12. Human Parasites

Topic

Humans can be infected with a variety of parasites.

Introduction

Like all living things, humans are susceptible to a wide range of *parasites*. Organisms that are classified as parasites spend most of their lives on, or within, a host from whom they receive nutrients and shelter. Parasites, such as the flea shown in Figure 1, that live on the outside of their hosts are *ectoparasites*. Those living within the bodies of their hosts are *endoparasites*, like the roundworm in Figure 2. Some parasites do very little damage to their hosts, while others weaken, or even kill, the organisms on which they live. Human parasites may be viruses, bacteria, fungi, protozoa, *arthropods,* or *helminthes*. The last two types of organisms are animals. Arthropods, which have a hard exoskeleton and jointed appendages, includes fleas and ticks. Helminthes are parasitic worms such as roundworms or tapeworms.

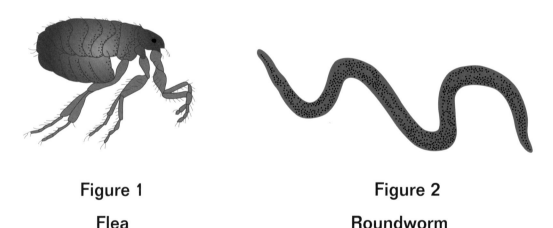

Figure 1	Figure 2
Flea	Roundworm

Endoparasites enter the body through the mouth or the skin. Those that invade through the mouth may remain in the intestine, or they can bore through the intestine to invade other tissues and organs. Parasites that penetrate the skin either bore directly through it or are introduced by the piercing mouth parts of insects.

Parasitic infections are the most dangerous, and common, disorders in some parts of the world. Because of this, scientists are constantly working to better understand how each parasite's life cycle can be disrupted. In this experiment, you will become an expert on one kind of human parasite.

Time Required

45 minutes for Part A
55 minutes for Part B

Materials

- ☞ access to the Internet
- ☞ colored pencils (or computer with printer)
- ☞ science notebook

Safety Note   Please review and follow the safety guidelines at the beginning of this volume.

Procedure, Part A

1. Select a human parasite to research from the list below.

   Acanthamoeba
   Ancylostoma duodenale
     (and/or *Necator americanus*)
   Ascaris lumbricoides
   Balantinium coli
   Cryptosporidium
   Dracunculus medinensis
   Entamoeba histolytica
   Enterobius vermicularis
   Fasciola hepatica
   Giardia lamblia
   Gnathostoma spinigerum
   Hymenolepis nana

   Leishmania
   Onchocerca volvulus
   Pediculosis (body lice)
   Plasmodium falciparum
   Taenia
   Toxocara
   Toxoplasma
   Trichinella
   Trypanosoma brucei
   Schistosoma mansoni (and/or
     S. *haematobium* and S.
     japonicum)
   Wuchereria bancrofti

2. Use the Internet to research the parasite you selected. Find all of the information requested on the data table and record your findings.

Data Table	
Topic	**Your notes**
Common name of parasite	
Name of disease caused by parasite (if applicable)	
Geographic regions where parasite is found	
Life cycle of parasite	
Type of organism (bacteria, protozoan, fungus, plant, animal)	
Symptoms of infection with the parasite	
Medical treatment for the parasite	

Procedure, Part B

1. Arrange your finding in an attractive brochure of your own design. Include at least two pictures in the brochure. Make the brochure neat, colorful, and informative. You may either write and draw the material for your brochure or use a computer and printer.

2. On the last page of your brochure, include your recommendations for eradicating this parasitic infection in humans.

3. Share your brochure with the class.

Analysis

1. In your own words, define *host*.
2. List three ways in which parasites affect their human hosts.
3. Explain why most parasitic infections are not fatal.
4. Warm, humid parts of the United States support more parasitic infections than cool, dry areas. Why do you think this is so?
5. How do you think that global warming could affect the spread of malaria, a disease spread by mosquitoes?

What's Going On?

Efforts to eliminate parasitic infections have taken many strategies. Malaria, one of the most common parasitic conditions, is a life-threatening disease that kills about 3,000 people a day. The parasite that causes malaria is transmitted by female anopheles mosquitoes. The best way to prevent malaria is to avoid being bitten. One highly effective prevention tool is a simple mosquito net that is put around bedding. However, malaria is still common. Once a person has been bitten, antimalarial medication must be taken to manage the disease.

One success story in the fight against parasitic infections is the virtual elimination of guinea worms. These animals require access to bodies of water such as streams or ponds because larvae of the worms live in water fleas (see Figure 3). When people drink the water, they consume the tiny fleas and become infected with guinea worms. After a female worm matures inside the body, she emerges from the host by boring her way out, causing extreme pain. Efforts to eliminate the parasite have focused on teaching people to sanitize their water supplies.

Connections

Parasites can exploit any part of the body. Each type of parasite is highly adapted for its particular niche. The *adaptations* shown by parasites vary, depending on where they live and how they get their food. For example, tapeworms are long and flat like ribbons, with suckers or hooks on their heads that make it possible for them to attach to the inside of this hosts' intestines. They do not need mouths or digestive systems because they absorb their hosts' digested food directly through their skin. Since they are surrounded by food and spend their adult lives in one location, they have no need for eyes or appendages. Intestinal flukes are small,

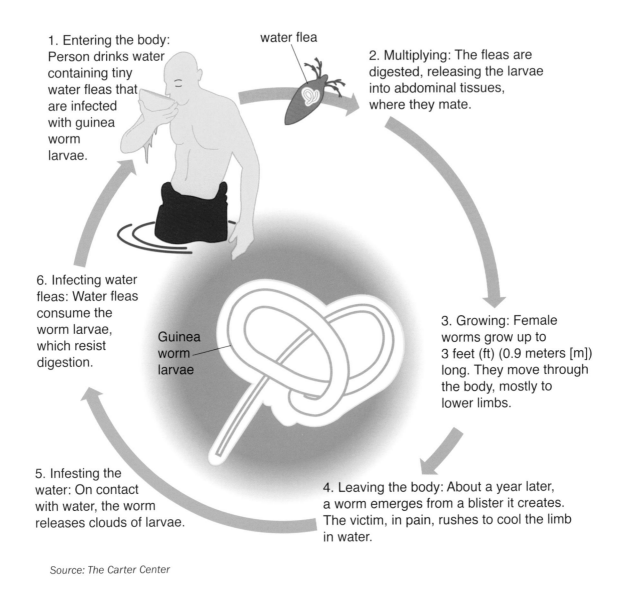

1. Entering the body: Person drinks water containing tiny water fleas that are infected with guinea worm larvae.

water flea

2. Multiplying: The fleas are digested, releasing the larvae into abdominal tissues, where they mate.

6. Infecting water fleas: Water fleas consume the worm larvae, which resist digestion.

Guinea worm larvae

3. Growing: Female worms grow up to 3 feet (ft) (0.9 meters [m]) long. They move through the body, mostly to lower limbs.

5. Infesting the water: On contact with water, the worm releases clouds of larvae.

4. Leaving the body: About a year later, a worm emerges from a blister it creates. The victim, in pain, rushes to cool the limb in water.

Source: The Carter Center

Figure 3

Life cycle of Guinea worms

flattened worms that attach to their hosts' tissues with suckers. The bodies of flukes are covered with thick cuticles to protect them from their hosts' strong digestive juices.

Want to Know More?

See appendix for Our Findings.

Further Reading

Carlo Denegri Foundation. "Atlas of Parasitology." Available online. URL: http://www.cdfound.to.it/html/atlas.htm. Accessed October 27, 2008. This Web site is an excellent collection of information on and photographs of parasites.

Centers for Disease Control and Prevention. "Parasitic Diseases." Available online. URL: http://www.cdc.gov/ncidod/dpd/parasites/ index.htm. Accessed October 27, 2008. This Web site provides detailed information about parasitic infections.

Krumhardt, Barbara. "Human Parasites." Available online. URL: http:// www.dmacc.cc.ia.us/instructors/human.htm. Accessed October 27, 2008. This Web site includes some great photographs of parasitic protozoans and worms.

13. Rocks and Minerals

Topic

Rocks are made up of several different minerals, each of which has a specific chemical composition.

Introduction

Rocks, mixtures of different kinds of minerals, are classified into three different types, depending on how they are formed. *Igneous rocks* form when magma (molten, hot rock) cools and solidifies. Magma comes from deep within the Earth, where heat and pressure are extremely high. *Sedimentary rocks* are made when igneous or metamorphic rock is broken or *weathered* into smaller pieces. Over time, the pieces of rocks and minerals are laid down on the Earth's surface. Eventually, they form layers that become cemented together. Like sedimentary rocks, *metamorphic rocks* are also made from preexisting rocks. In this case, the rocks have been subjected to heat or pressure and deposited in swirls, layers, or folds. Metamorphic rocks that become extremely hot are changed into igneous rock. The conversion of rock material into different types is referred to the *rock cycle* (see Figure 1).

A rock might be made up of several different types of *minerals*, naturally occurring, crystalline substances that have characteristic chemical compositions. *Crystals* are geometric solids whose atoms are arranged in definite, repeating patterns. Several types of crystals are shown in Figure 2. The ordered atomic structure of a mineral gives it unique physical characteristics. In this experiment, you will research one of the minerals that make up rocks.

Time Required

two 55-minute periods

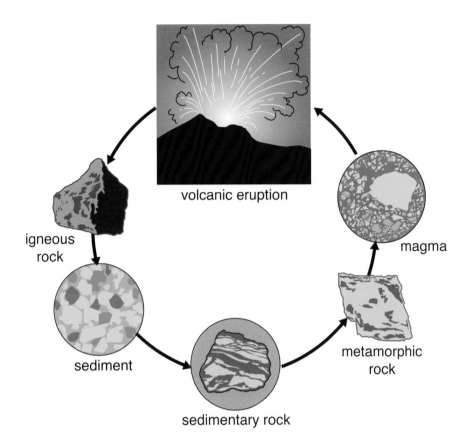

volcanic eruption

igneous
rock

magma

sediment

metamorphic
rock

sedimentary rock

Figure 1

The rock cycle

Figure 2

Minerals occur in a variety of shapes and colors.

Materials

➥   access to the Internet

➥   stiff paper or poster board

➥   scissors

➥   glue

➥   tape

➥   science notebook

Safety Note   Please review and follow the safety guidelines at the beginning of this volume.

Procedure

1.   Select a mineral from the list below.

Apatite	Corundum	Muscovite
Augite	Cuprite	Olivine
Azurite	Diamond	Quartz
Barite	Dolomite	Serpentine
Bauxite	Fluorite	Pyrite
Beryl	Galena	Silver
Biotite	Garnet	Sulfur
Calcite	Glauconite	Talc
Chalcocite	Gold	Titanite
Chromite	Graphite	Topaz
Cinnabar	Gypsum	Turquoise
Copper	Halite	Zoisite

2.   Access the Internet and research the mineral you selected. Record you findings in your science notebook. You will use your findings to create an informative cube and to answer the Analysis questions.

3.   Create a cube. To do so:

    a. Trace the pattern for the cube (Figure 3) onto the stiff paper.

    b. Cut the cube pattern along the dotted lines.

    c. Fold the cube on the solid lines.

    d. Glue or tape the cube together.

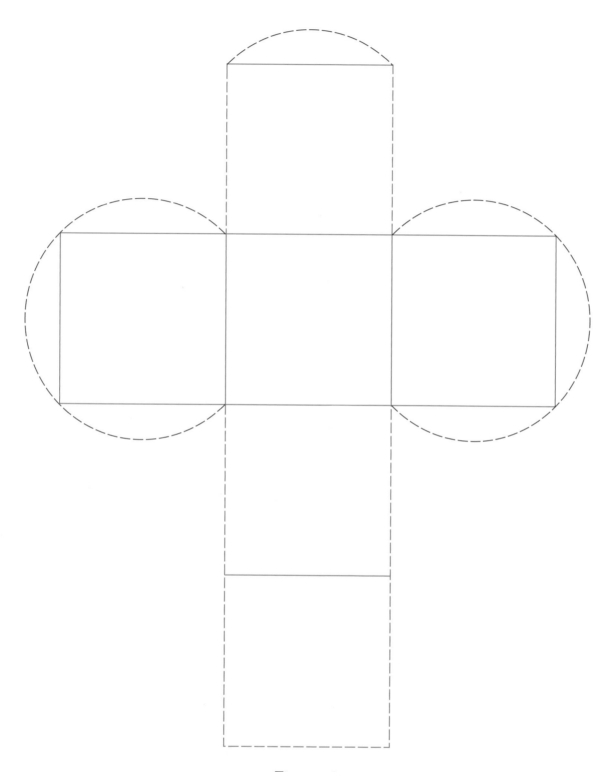

Figure 3

Pattern for cube

4. The cube has six sides. Arrange your research on the sides of the cube as follows:

Side 1: Name; chemical formula

Side 2: Color

Side 3: Places where it is found

Side 4: Uses

Side 5: Hardness and specific gravity

Side 6: Luster and streak

Analysis

1. In your own words, explain how a mineral might travel through the rock cycle.

2. What is the difference between a rock and a mineral?

3. What elements make up the mineral you researched?

4. Opals are beautiful pieces of stone that are used to make jewelry. Opals are naturally occurring solids that lack an orderly, internal structure. Would you classify opals as minerals? Why or why not?

5. Write a one-sentence description of the physical characteristics of your mineral.

What's Going On?

Experts estimate that there are about 2,000 different kinds of minerals on Earth. However, only about 20 of these minerals are common and 10 of them make up 90 percent of the planet's crust. Most minerals are chemical compounds, but a few, such as copper, silver, gold, and lead are elements. The most common group of minerals is the silicates, compounds of the two most common elements on Earth, oxygen and silicon. Silicates are identified by their unique characteristics: they are not opaque, not soluble in acid, and lightweight. Quartz is a familiar silicate. Others are olivine, a gemstone, and mica, which early settlers used to cover their windows.

The other types of minerals, the nonsilicates, include carbonates, oxides, sulfides, phosphates, and salts. Carbonates are transparent, have an characteristic density, and are soluble in acidic solutions. Limestone rock is made from carbonates. Oxides are a diverse group that includes both hard and soft minerals whose colors vary from pale to black. Iron oxide, or magnetite, is a naturally magnetic compound. Sulfides are generally metallic and opaque, with average hardness and high density. Many sulfides, such as silver, lead, and copper sulfides, are economically important. Phosphates are a variable group with generally strong color and above average density. The phosphate apatite is found in the bones and teeth of all vertebrates. Salts are compounds made of a metal and a nonmetal. Sodium chloride, or common table salt, is an important compound in the diets of all animals.

Connections

From lightbulbs to toothpaste to breakfast cereal, we use minerals everyday. Light bulbs contain glass, which is made from silica, limestone, coal, and salt. Wires in incandescent light bulbs are made from tungsten, copper, nickel, and molybdenum. Toothpaste contains abrasive minerals such as aluminum, limestone, and silica to rub plaque from teeth. Many types of toothpaste have fluoride to help strength tooth enamel. The white color of the paste, as well as the sparkle seen in some products is due to minerals. Because we must have several minerals in our diets to stay healthy, a balanced diet is essential. Iron, a mineral we get from eating red meat, helps our bodies make red blood cells. Calcium, which comes from milk and other dairy products, is needed in the construction of bones and teeth as well as in the transmission of nerve impulses. Other major minerals in the diet are phosphorus, magnesium, sodium, potassium, chloride, and sulfur. Minerals that we need in only trace amounts include manganese, copper, iodine, zinc, cobalt, fluoride, and selenium.

 ## Want to Know More?

See appendix for Our Findings.

Further Reading

Annenberg Media. "Interactives Rock Cycles," 2008. Available online. URL: http://www.learner.org/interactives/rockcycle/about.html. Accessed October 15, 2008. Students work their way through the interactive information on this Web site to learn about rock formation.

Geology.com, 2008. Available online. URL: http://geology.com. Accessed November 11, 2008. This extensive Web site provides news, links, graphics, and information on rock and mineral collections.

Rock Hounds. "Discover How Rocks Are Formed," January 29, 1999. Available online. URL: http://www.fi.edu/fellows/payton/rocks/create/. Accessed October 15, 2008. This Web site shows animations of how each type of rock is formed.

14. Breathing Demonstration

Topic

The mechanics of breathing can be demonstrated using a model.

Introduction

You may rarely think about it, but breathing is an activity you carry out about 20 times a minute. Breathing is one step in *respiration*, a two-phase process that gets oxygen into the blood and removes carbon dioxide. Your respiratory system, shown in Figure 1, pulls air into the lungs. The oxygen within inhaled air diffuses across lung tissue into the blood, which carries it to cells. Within cells, the next step of respiration takes place. Internal or *cellular respiration* is the chemical process in which glucose combines with oxygen to produce the energy that runs cells. Carbon dioxide gas produced during cellular respiration is delivered to the lungs by the blood. When you exhale, you expel this unwanted gas.

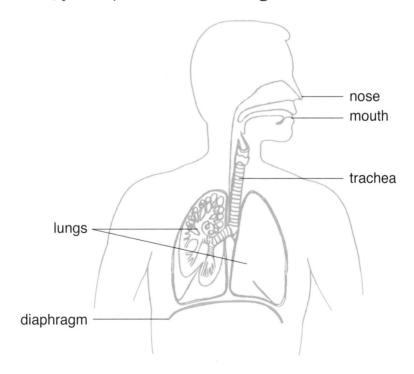

Figure 1

The part of the body that handles external respiration is the respiratory system. Air enters the respiratory system because of differences in air pressure inside and outside the lungs. In this experiment, you will carry out research to find out why air enters and leaves the lungs, then develop a model that demonstrates the principles of breathing.

Time Required

two 55-minute periods

Materials

- access to the Internet
- scissors
- glue
- tape
- metric ruler
- stiff paper
- rubber bands
- empty 2-liter bottle
- small plastic trash bag
- drinking straw
- balloons
- clay
- science notebook

Safety Note   Please review and follow the safety guidelines at the beginning of this volume.

Procedure

1. Access the Internet and carry out searches to learn about the structures of the respiratory system. Use what you learn to help you answer Analysis questions 1 through 6.

2. While conducting your research, find drawings of the lungs that demonstrate the role of air pressure in inhaling and exhaling. Sketch the drawings in your science notebook. Label all parts of the drawings and explain what is happening in each.

3. Based on your research and your sketches, create a working model of a lung, using the materials provided by your teacher. Your model must meet the following criteria:
   a. The trachea, lung, and diaphragm must be represented.
   b. The model "lung" must inflate because of a change in air pressure.
   c. The model "lung" must deflate because of a change in air pressure.

4. Answer Analysis questions 7 through 9.

Analysis

1. Describe the path that air follows from outside the body into the lungs.
2. Describe an *alveolus*. What is its function?
3. What is the diaphragm? What is its function?
4. When the diaphragm contracts, the rib cage is pushed up and outward. Does this cause air to move into or out of the lungs? Why?
5. When the diaphragm relaxes, it moves upward in the rib cage. Does this cause air to move into or out of the lungs? Why?
6. How does *Boyle's law* help explain lung function?
7. In your model, what represents the trachea? What represents the lung? What represents the diaphragm?
8. How does your model demonstrate the inflation of a lung?
9. How does your model show the role of Boyle's law in inhaling and exhaling?

What's Going On?

When you inhale, air moves from the environment into your lungs. This movement of air is a passive process in which air flows from an area of high pressure to an area of low pressure. Inhaling causes the rib cage to expand, increasing the space in the chest and allowing the lungs to expand (see Figure 2). As the volume of the lungs increases, the air pressure within them decreases, a phenomenon explained by Boyle's law. According to Boyle, an increase in volume of a gas reduces pressure. Air travels naturally from regions of high pressure to low.

When you exhale, the diaphragm relaxes and moves upward, reducing the size of the chest cavity and the volume of the lungs. When lung volume decreases, air pressure within the lungs increases. Air moves from inside the lungs to outside where pressure is lower.

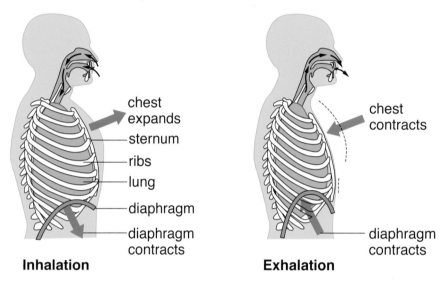

Inhalation   **Exhalation**

Figure 2

Connections

Any condition or disease that interferes with the lungs' ability to expand or with the function of alveoli causes serious breathing problems. One such condition is a *pneumothorax*, an accumulation of air in the space outside the lungs. Air builds up in the pleural space, the area between the lung and chest wall, preventing the lung from expanding. As a result, the lung collapses and puts pressure on the heart and other lung. Symptoms of pneumothorax include chest pain and shortness of breath. Treatment for a large pneumothorax is insertion of a tube into the pleural space to drain off the air. This treatment allows the deflated lung to re-inflate and removes pressure on the heart and other lung. Causes of pneumothorax include injuries that penetrate the lungs as well as tumors, infections, or objects blocking the airway.

Pneumonia is a general term for any infection of alveoli due to a pathogen, such as bacteria, virus, or fungus. Infecting organisms are usually inhaled, but they can be carried to lungs by the bloodstream. Symptoms of pneumonia include a cough that produces *sputum*, thick mucus, as well as fever and mild chest pain. Treatment involves deep-breathing exercises, medications, such as antibiotics, and supplemental oxygen if needed.

Want to Know More?

See appendix for Our Findings.

Further Reading

American Lung Association. "Your Lungs," 2008. Available online. URL: http://www.lungusa.org/site/c.duLUK9OOE/b.22551/k.F8CD/Your_Lwys. htm. Accessed November 8, 2008. An animation on this Web site explains how the lungs work.

Freudenrich, Craig. "How Your Lungs Work?" How Stuff Works. Available online. URL: http://health.howstuffworks.com/lung2.htm. Accessed November 7, 2008. This Web site provides good graphics as well as simple explanations of gas exchange and lung function.

Lamb, Annette, and Larry Johnson. "Respiratory System," December 2001. Available online. URL: http://42explore.com/respsyst.htm. Accessed November 8, 2008. This Web site gives links to dozens of great sites on respiratory function.

15. Nanoscale Science

Topic

Nanoscale science is conducted on the microscopic level.

Introduction

Nanoscale science, or nanoscience, is an extension of regular sciences into the study of very small objects. In units of time or length, the prefix "nano" means one-billionth of that unit. Therefore, a nanometer (nm), is one-billionth of a meter (m), or 10^{-9} m. Most nanoscience work involves materials that are smaller than 100 nm.

To put the nanoscale into perspective, take a closer look at the measurements used in distance. If you extend your right arm straight out from the side of your body, the distance from your nose to your fingertips is about one meter (m). One thousandth of a m is a millimeter (mm), about the width of penny. One thousandth of a mm is a micron (μm), which is too small to see with the naked eye. A bacterial cell is about 1 μm in diameter (see Figure 1). A nanometer (nm) is one thousandth of a μm. This means that there are one billion nm in 1 m.

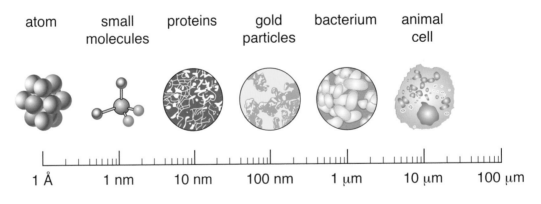

| atom | small molecules | proteins | gold particles | bacterium | animal cell |

1 Å   1 nm   10 nm   100 nm   1 μm   10 μm   100 μm

Figure 1

To get some perspective on nanoscales, consider these examples. Several water molecules would be required to fill a sphere with a diameter of 1 nm. A DNA helix has a diameter of about 2 nm. Proteins, carbohydrates, and fats are molecules with nanoscale dimensions. To study materials so small, scientists rely on tiny measurements. To gain some insight into this dimension, you will carry out Internet research to learn more about nanoscale science.

Time Required

55 minutes

Materials

➡ access to the Internet

➡ science notebook

Safety Note   Please review and follow the safety guidelines at the beginning of this volume.

Procedure

1. Access the National Science Foundation's "Nanoscience" Web site http://www.nsf.gov/news/overviews/nano/index.jsp. Read the articles on this Web site and answer Analysis questions 1 through 7.

2. Go to "How Can I Learn More" on the main menu. Under Frequently Asked Questions, "What Is a Nanometer," select "The Size of Nano." scroll to the bottom of the page and select "The Scale of Things." Answer Analysis questions 8 through 10

3. On the page of Frequently Asked Questions, examine the menu on the left side. Select "Resources" and then "Links."

4. Review the work being done at various research centers around the world. After reviewing the work, select a topic that interests you. Write a paragraph in your science notebook summarizing this topic.

Analysis

1. What is one nanometer?

2. Give the measurements of the following in nm: thickness of paper; one gold atom; a black hair; a hemoglobin protein.

3. Why do scientists study materials at the nanoscale level?

4. How does the surface area of nanoscale materials compare to the surface area of larger-scale materials?

5. Describe a unique behavior of gold on the nanoscale level.

6. What are some properties of carbon nanotubes? Describe some future uses of carbon nanotubes.

7. Name several fields or industries that use nanoscale materials.

8. Complete the following statements:

   a. 1 cm is equal to 10 _____ or 10^{-2} _____.

   b. 1 mm is equal to _____ nm or _____ meters.

   c. 0.1 mm is equal to _____ nm or _____ meters.

   d. 1,000 nm equals _____ μm or 10^{-6} m.

   e. 10^{-8} m equals 10 _____.

   f. 10^{-9} m equal 1 _____.

9. A dust mite is 200 μm wide. What is the size of the dust mite in nanometers?

10. Which is larger, the head of a pin or a pollen grain?

What's Going On?

All of the natural world is built of materials on the nanoscale level. Atoms create molecules, which are the building blocks of organic compounds, such as carbohydrates, and inorganic materials like minerals. Humans have only been able to view and manipulate molecules and atoms since the advent of high-power microscopes and equipment that can interface with these tiny particles.

Currently, nanoscale work is primarily research. In one research project, scientists copied the nanostructure of the leaves of the lotus plant or water lily (see Figure 2), a species that has the ability to self-clean. The molecular make-up of lotus leaves enables them to keep off dust particles that would otherwise cover the leaves and slow photosynthesis. Scientists created a similar structure made of plastic in which molecules are shaped and arranged like the lotus molecules (see Figure 3). When water hits the molecules, it rolls off. Layers of these molecules used to make waterproof fabric. Another research group is deciphering the structure of spider webs, which are extremely strong but highly flexible. Their goal is use nanoscale crystals to produce artificial fibers with these same characteristics. Another product that has resulted from nanoscale research is the magnetoresistance head that is used to increase the storage capacity of computer hard drives. Materials have also been developed that can be used to treat burns and wounds.

Figure 2

Lotus plant

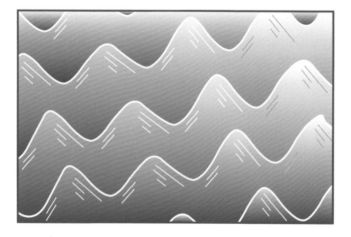

Figure 3

Nanoscale view of self-cleaning plastic modeled on the lotus leaf

Connections

The future of nanoscale technology includes expansion in every field of science and engineering. Scientists predict that nanoscience will develop electricity-producing solar cells that can be embedded in siding and roofing. These cells would provide residences with electricity from a source that does not produce air-polluting gases. The automobile industry is exploring nanoscience to develop tires that are longer lasting and skid resistant. This same technology can also be applied to other products such as the belts in car engines as well as footwear and athletic apparel. In the field of pharmacology, scientists hope to develop medications that can be implanted and delivered to the body in small doses over time. They are also researching molecules that can be used to tag or label cancer cells, making them easier to treat. Other arenas that are actively involved in nanoscale products are the fields of defense and computer electronics. Only the imagination of scientists and engineers will limit this fast-growing field.

Want to Know More?

See appendix for Our Findings.

Further Reading

Institute of Nanotechnology. "What Is Nanotechnology?" 2007. Available online. URL: http://www.nano.org.uk/whatis.htm. Accessed November 15, 2008. The institute's Web site has links to images, reports, and news related to nanoscience.

National Nanotechnology Initiative. "Nanotechnology, Big Things From a Tiny World." Available online. URL: http://www.nano.gov/Nanotechnology_BigThingsfromaTinyWorldspread.pdf. Accessed November 16, 2008. This brochure explains the world in simple terms using colorful graphics.

Parry-Hill, Matthew J., Christopher A. Burdett, and Michael W. Davidson. "Molecular Expressions, Science, Optics, and You," September 26, 2007. Available online. URL: http://micro.magnet.fsu.edu/primer/java/scienceopticsu/powersof10/. Accessed November 15, 2008. Through an interactive Java tutorial, one can experience the dimensions of the universe and those of an atom.

16. How Are Caves Formed?

Topic

Caves can be formed by water, lava, and the action of bacteria.

Introduction

A natural opening in the Earth that is large enough for a person to enter is a *cave*. Within some caves, beautiful cave formations or *speleothems*, structures such as *stalactites* and *stalagmites,* rise from the floor and hang from the ceilings. Stalactites are calcium carbonate formations that hang down while stalagmites build up on the floor due to an accumulation of calcium carbonate. In many cases these two meet and form tall columns (see Figure 1).

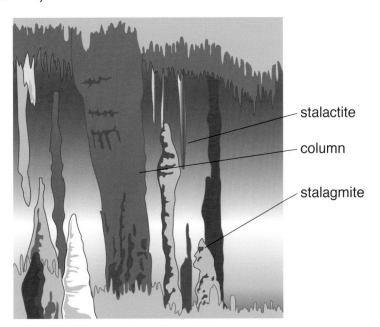

stalactite

column

stalagmite

Figure 1

Caves are classified into two big groups according to how they were formed. Those that developed as the host rock was solidifying are *primary caves*. Primary caves are most often found in old flows of lava. *Secondary caves* were created after the host rock was formed. In these cases, soluble rock such as limestone, dolomite, or marble was carved out over millions of years. Most caves are of the secondary type and were formed by the action of acidic water.

Water can become acidified to form either carbonic acid or sulfuric acid. Weakly acidic carbonic acid (H_2CO_3) is formed when precipitation dissolves carbon dioxide (CO_2) in the air. This water percolates through the ground, dissolving other compounds to form a slightly stronger acidic solution that erodes limestone and other soluble rocks (see Figure 2). Sulfuric acid is formed when hydrogen sulfide gas from deep in the Earth moves up through cracks in the crust until it encounters the water table. A solution of hydrogen sulfide and water creates sulfuric acid. In this experiment, you will conduct research to learn the details of cave formation and you will present information on a specific cave to the class.

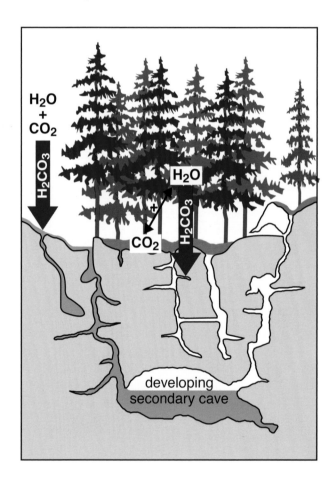

Figure 2

Time Required

90 minutes

Materials

- ☞ access to the Internet
- ☞ color printer or colored markers
- ☞ poster board
- ☞ science notebook

Safety Note   Please review and follow the safety guidelines at the beginning of this volume.

Procedure

1. Access the Internet and go to "How Caves Form" by Rick Goreau at http://www.pbs.org/wgbh/nova/caves/form.html. Click on the animation link titled "How Caves Form." Select each of the four ways in which caves form and read the information about each.

2. Answer Analysis questions 1 through 11.

3. Go to the article on caveology on the Onondoga Cave State Park Web site at http://www.mostateparks.com/onondaga/cavesformed.htm. Read the article and answer Analysis questions 12 through 15.

4. Select a cave or cavern to research. You may use one of the famous caves listed on the data table below or choose another one you know about.

5. Create a poster about the cave you investigated. Your poster should be neat and colorful, and it should include the cave's location and features as well as explaining how the cave was formed.

Data Table	
Famous Caves	
Carlsbad Caverns	Pierre Saint Martin
Mammoth Cave	Altamira
Castleguard Cave	Grotte des Demoiselles
Lascaux Caves	Ochtinska Aragonite Cave
Dan yr Ogof Cave	Hölloch Caverns
Blue Grotto	Cuevas del Drach
Eisriesenwelt	

Analysis

1. What are the most numerous types of caves?

2. How is carbonic acid formed?

3. How far does rainwater seep into limestone?

4. What effect does carbonic acid have on the limestone?

5. When do stalactites and stalagmites appear in limestone caves?

6. How can moving water create caves?

7. How do waves create caves?

8. How does lava form a cave?

9. What are extremophiles?

10. What gas do extremophiles produce?

11. How does this gas contribute to cave formation?

12. How was Onondaga Cave formed?

13. What is the source of the rock that makes up Onondaga Cave?

14. Write the chemical equation that shows how carbonic acid is formed.

15. How does carbonic acid affect limestone and dolomite?

What's Going On?

Most of the caves in the United States are clustered in specific regions. These regions have geological features in common and are classified as *karst* landscapes. A karst is a geographic area that is made of soluble rock such as limestone, dolomite, marble, or gypsum. About 20 percent of the U.S. landscape is comprised of karst regions. Besides caves, these regions have features such as sinkholes, disappearing streams, and pits.

Karsts also contain *aquifers*, large reservoirs of water, beneath the surface. Aquifers are filled by rainwater that percolates through the soil. When water reaches the aquifer, it travels through two zones. The first is the *zone of aeration*, an area just above the water table where most of the spaces in rocks are filled with air. The next section is the *zone of saturation,* where the rock is completely saturated with water. Between these two zones is the *capillary fringe* (see Figure 3). Cave passages that contain air are within the zone of aeration, but cave-forming processes occur in both regions.

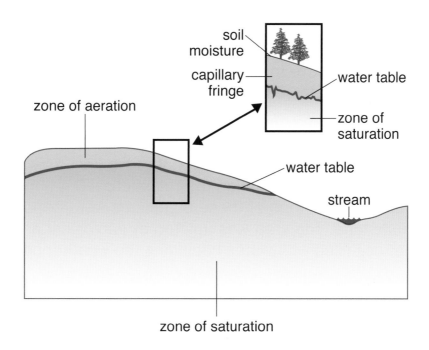

Figure 3

Water that percolates through the soil into an aquifer is slightly acidic because it has combined with carbon dioxide in the air and with acidic compounds in the soil. This acidified water eats away at the soluble rock, especially at the region of the water table. Over time, when the water table recedes, the caves are exposed to air for the first time. At this stage, stalactites and stalagmites begin form.

Stalactites hang from the ceiling like icicles. Each structure begins as a single drop of acidified water that carries dissolved calcium compounds. As the drop hangs suspended from the cave ceiling, the water evaporates, leaving behind calcium carbonate and calcite. A second drop develops on this deposit, eventually adding its dissolved minerals. Over thousands of years, large stalactites form. Stalagmites are built from the cave floor upward. Water drips from stalactites, leaving tiny deposits of dissolved calcium compounds on the cave floor. When the water evaporates, only the minerals are left behind. These build up slowly, forming impressive structures. If the stalagmite is able to grow for long enough, it eventually merges with its parent stalactite to form a column.

Connections

Carlsbad Caverns in New Mexico is one of the largest caves in the United States. This cave is made up of an enormous tunnel of caverns and includes more than 84 large rooms, many of them featuring dramatic limestone formations. Archeological evidence shows that nomadic hunters and gatherers used the cave for shelter. The same caverns were visited by Spanish explorers in the 1500s.

About 250 million years ago, the area of these caverns was an inland sea. Near the shore, a massive reef of lime-secreting organisms like corals and sponges formed. The reef grew for millions of years until it was hundreds of feet thick and more than four miles (6.4 kilometers [km]) long. When the sea dried up, the skeletons of these organisms were deposited and pressed into limestone. The area was uplifted by geological processes and fractures in the rock filled with water, beginning the weathering process.

Much of the dissolution that produced Carlsbad Caverns was due to more than carbonic acid. Sulfuric acid, a much stronger compound, played an important role. Near this uplifted seabed are regions that are rich in oil fields. Hydrogen sulfide gas from these regions migrated up through the limestone floor toward the water table, where it combined with water to form sulfuric acid. It was the action of this strong acid that created the large rooms characteristic of Carlsbad. Eventually, the water table dropped and the caves drained, leaving the large rooms exposed.

 Want to Know More?

See appendix for Our Findings.

Further Reading

Cornish, Jim. Gander's Academy, 2000. Available online. URL: http://www.stemnet.nf.ca/CITE/cave.htm. Accessed November 16, 2008. On this Web site, Cornish answers basic questions about cave structure.

Speleological Union of Ireland. "Caves and Karst: How Are They Formed?" Available online. URL: http://caving.ie/caving/formation.php. Accessed December 5, 2008. This Web site explains how caves are formed, how their shapes are sculpted, and how speleothems are created.

University of Texas at Austin. "How Caves Form." Available online. URL: http://www.esi.utexas.edu/outreach/caves/caves.php. Accessed December 6, 2008. Secondary cave formation is explained and cave-related terms are defined on this Web site.

17. Sunspots and the Solar Cycle

Topic

The frequency of sunspots varies with regular solar cycles.

Introduction

The Sun may look like a uniform glowing orb, but its surface is always changing. The appearance of the Sun is affected by its constantly changing magnetic fields. *Sunspots* are planet-size dark areas on the Sun that result from changes in the Sun's magnetic field. A sunspot lasts for a few days before disappearing. The frequency of sunspots increases and decreases on a regular cycle. This *solar cycle* fluctuates from the time when the Sun has a minimum number of spots to the time when it has the maximum number. The lengths of solar cycles vary, but average about 11 years (see Figure 1). During the *solar maximum*, the time when sunspots are frequent, 100 to 200 sunspots may occur in a year. In a *solar minimum*, astronomers may view less than a dozen in one year.

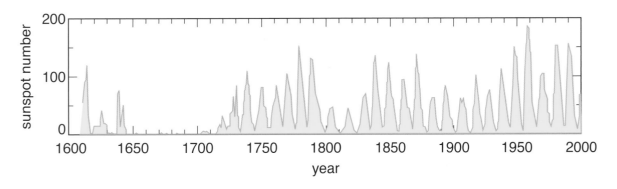

Figure 1

Yearly averaged sunspot numbers, 1610–2000

When the solar cycle is at its maximum, more solar events, such as *coronal mass ejections* and *solar flares*, occur. These episodes are caused by sudden, dramatic changes in the Sun's magnetic fields. During ejections and flares, energized particles of matter are flung into space, some traveling toward Earth. Energized particles can interfere with communication devices and the generation of electrical power. In this experiment, you will learn more about sunspots and the solar cycle.

Time Required

45 minutes

Materials

➥   access to the Internet

➥   science notebook

Safety Note   Please review and follow the safety guidelines at the beginning of this volume.

Procedure

1. Go to the National Oceanic and Atmospheric Association (NOAA) Web site titled "A Primer on Space Weather" at http://www.swpc. noaa.gov/primer/primer.html. Use this site to help you answer Analysis questions 1 through 12.

2. Go to the Australian government's Web site, "Communications and Space Weather," http://www.ips.gov.au/Educational/1/3/4. Read sections 1 through 3.1 and answer Analysis questions 13 through 19.

3. Scientists photograph the Sun at regular intervals and analyze the photographs to determine the number of sunspots. Areas of sunspots appear as contrasting light and dark areas. Figure 2 shows two regions of sunspots. Go to the most recent sunspot images at http://sohowww.nascom.nasa.gov/data/realtime-images. html. Find the gray image, which is titled "MDI Magnetogram." Below the gray image, locate the link titled "More MDI Magnetogram." Click on this link to find images of the Sun's surface taken over the last several days.

    a. Click on the first image to enlarge it. Note the time and date and record these on the data table. Count the number of sunspots on this image and record the number on the data table.

b. Repeat step 4 until you have viewed all of the images. Extend the data table if necessary.

c. Answer Analysis questions 20 and 21.

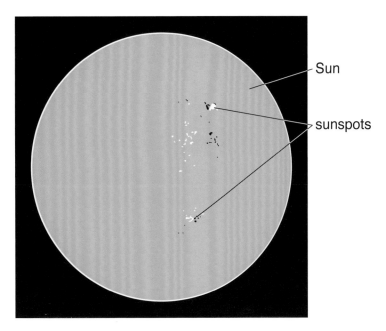

Figure 2

Data Table		
Date	**Time**	**Number of sunspots**

4. Extend your research to find out how the solar maximum and minimum affect radio and satellite communications.

Analysis

1. How much energy does the Sun generate?

2. A single second of the Sun's energy could power the activities on Earth for _____ years.

3. What is the source of the Sun's energy?

4. How long does it take energy produced in the core of the Sun to reach the Sun's surface?

5. How long has the Sun been producing energy? How long will it continue to do so?

6. How will the Sun change in the future?

7. What are sunspots?

8. What causes sunspots?

9. What is the cycle of sunspot occurrence?

10. What is the cause of coronal mass ejections?

11. What are solar flares?

12. What are coronal holes?

13. What is space weather?

14. What causes space weather?

15. How does space weather affect Earth's ionosphere?

16. What is the name of the current solar cycle? When did it begin?

17. What was the largest number of sunspots recorded in a cycle?

18. Where is the ionosphere?

19. How does the density of the F layer of the atmosphere affect communications?

20. What is the maximum number of sunspots you saw on the magnetographs?

21. Based on the magnetographs that you viewed, would you say that the Sun in currently in a solar minimum or a solar maximum?

What's Going On?

Although the solar cycle averages about 11 years, it varies. At the maximum, the Sun's surface is freckled with spots, and the star spews billions of tons of electrified gas toward Earth. All of these charged particles in our upper atmosphere produce spectacular colored light shows at night in extreme northern and southern regions. However, the particles also disrupt radio signals, satellite signals, and electrical production. During the minimum, spots are absent and few radio transmission problems occur.

The most recent solar cycle was unusually short, with a maximum in 2000 and a minimum in 2006. For several months in 2006, no sunspots were observed. By late 2008, one or two sunspots could be seen on most days. The next maximum is expected sometime between 2010 and 2012. Some scientists predict that this period will be the most active in the last 50 years.

Connections

Sunspots appear as dark regions on the Sun's surface. Because sunspots are extremely large, they were observed long before telescopes were invented. Early astronomers even noted that sunspots move across the Sun's surface over a period of several days. The German astronomer Johannes Kepler (1571–1630) noticed sunspots in 1607, but he mistook them for Mercury, which he thought was traveling in front of the Sun. A year later, telescopes were invented and many astronomers became interested in this solar phenomenon. Galileo Galilei (1564–1642), Italian mathematician, astronomer, and physicist, was one of the first to argue that the spots were part of the Sun, not a planet traveling in front of the star as Kepler had thought. Galileo's sketches of the Sun's surface indicate that many of his observations occurred during a solar maximum. Working independently, Christoph Scheiner (1573–1650), a German astronomer, carefully documented the movement of sunspots across the Sun's surface. Scheiner's study involved more than 2,000 observations of sunspots. Scheiner disagreed with Galileo arguing that the spots were not part of the Sun but were shadows caused by satellites of the Sun. Work by later astronomers supported Galileo's opinions.

Want to Know More?

See appendix for Our Findings.

Further Reading

McKee, Maggie. "'Maverick' Sunspot Heralds New Solar Cycle,"
New Scientist, January 07, 2008. Available online. URL: http://www.
newscientist.com/article/dn13153. Accessed March 25, 2009. The next
solar cycle is beginning with an unusual sunspot.

Phillips, Tony. "Solar Minimum Has Arrived," NASA, March 6, 2006.
Available online. URL: http://www.nasa.gov/vision/universe/solarsystem/
06mar_solarminimum.html. Accessed November 22, 2008. Phillips
explains what happened when the most recent solar minimum occurred.

Solar and Heliospheric Observatory. "Our Star the Sun," August 17, 2007.
Available online. URL: http://sohowww.nascom.nasa.gov/classroom/
classroom.html. Accessed November 19, 2008. Supported by the
European Space Agency and NASA, this Web site provides information on
the Sun and sunspots.

18. Types of Chemical Bonds

Topic

Elements form compounds through ionic and covalent bonding.

Introduction

Examination of the periodic table reveals that there are just over 100 elements. However, atoms of these elements can join in countless combinations to produce hundreds of chemically distinct substances. Atoms bond because the total energy of the combination is lower than the energy of the separated atoms. The compounds that result from bonded atoms are chemically and physically different than the elements from which they are formed.

Atoms can form two basic types of bonds: *ionic bonds* and *covalent bonds*. The type of bonding depends on the arrangement of electrons within the atoms involved. In ionic bonding, two elements join because electrons of one element are transferred to the other element. As a result, two *ions*, or charged particles, are formed. One ion contains extra electrons and has a negative charge, while the other has lost one or more electrons and has a positive charge. These two oppositely charged particles are attracted to each other. For example, during the reaction of sodium with chlorine, an electron from sodium is transferred to chlorine (see Figure 1). As a result sodium loses one electron and becomes a positive ion. Chlorine gains an electron and becomes a negative ion. The two ions are attracted to each other and form a bond that creates sodium chloride, or table salt.

Covalent bonds are formed when atoms share electrons. Sharing creates strong, stable compounds. The simplest example of covalent bonding occurs between two hydrogen atoms when they combine. Each hydrogen atom is made up of one proton and one electron. However, this is an unstable electron arrangement because two electrons are needed to make a hydrogen atom stable and unreactive. When two hydrogen atoms share their electrons, they form *diatomic* hydrogen gas, or H_2. In this experiment, you will conduct research on the Internet to learn more about bonding.

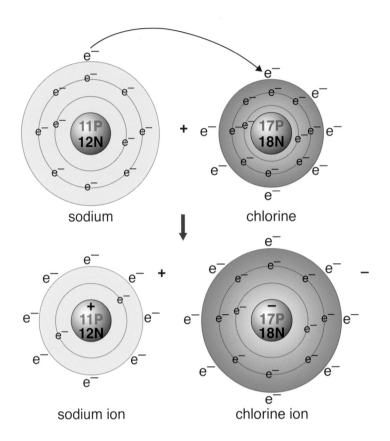

Figure 1

Time Required

45 minutes

Materials

- ⚬ access to Internet
- ⚬ science notebook

Safety Note   Please review and follow the safety guidelines at the beginning of this volume.

Procedure

1. Go to the Basic Chemistry Web site by Dr. June Steinberg at http://www2.nl.edu/jste/atomic.htm. Read the introduction and the

section titled "Energy Shells" to find out the role of outer shell electrons in chemical bonds.

2. Answer Analysis questions 1 through 6.

3. Go to the Chemical Bonds Web site by Dr. June Steinberg at http:// www2.nl.edu/jste/bonds.htm. Read the entire page and answer Analysis questions 7 through 16.

4. Go to Mr. Kent's Web site at http://www.kentchemistry.com/links/ bonding/bondingflashes/bond_types.swf. Click on each bond type to see an animation explaining how the bonds form. Answer Analysis question 17.

Analysis

1. What are the three basic components of atoms?

2. Where are electrons located?

3. Which energy shell contains the most energy, the innermost shell or the outermost shell?

4. Use the 2-8-8 rule to explain how 12 electrons will be distributed in an atom's energy shells.

5. What are the three ways in which atoms can fill their outer shells with a stable number of electrons?

6. Define *ion*.

7. How are ionic bonds and covalent bonds formed?

8. Explain what happens in the animation that shows how sodium and chlorine ions are formed.

9. At the end of the animation, what is the condition of the outer shells of the sodium and chloride ions?

10. Why do sodium and chloride ions form bonds?

11. Explain what happens in the animation showing the formation of a covalent bond.

12. After the animation, how many electrons will each hydrogen atom have in its outermost shell?

13. What is the difference between a nonpolar and a polar covalent bond?

14. Water is a polar molecule. In water, the oxygen atom attracts electrons more strongly than the smaller, weaker hydrogen atoms.

Draw a water molecule and show the slight negative and positive charges.

15. What type of bonds form between water molecules?

16. Arrange the three types of bonds, ionic, covalent, and hydrogen, in order from strongest to weakest.

17. After watching the animations at Mr. Kent's Web site, summarize what you learned about each type of bond.

What's Going On?

Stable or *inert* atoms are unreactive because they have a complete set of *valence electrons*, those in the outermost energy shells. Atoms that naturally have a stable electron configuration are the *noble gases*. Atoms of the noble gases have eight electrons in their outer energy levels, a configuration known as an *octet.* Other atoms, those that have incomplete sets of valence electrons, can reach a stable, noble gas configuration by losing or gaining electrons.

Atoms that have one, two, or three valence electrons are most likely to lose these to reach a stable octet. For example, sodium, located on the left side of the periodic table, has only one valence electron, which it can easily give up. Chlorine, on the opposite end of the period table, has seven valence electrons. The easiest way for chlorine to reach the noble gas configuration is to gain one electron. The transfer of an electron from sodium to chlorine creates two ions of opposite charges. The ions are held together by the attractive forces.

Atoms that have four valence electrons are likely to share with other atoms. Carbon, for example, has four valence electrons and can share these with four other carbon atoms, or with atoms of hydrogen and oxygen. Silicon also has four valence electrons, explaining why it easily forms covalent bonds with oxygen and with other silicon atoms.

The periodic table can be used to determine the number of valence electrons in an atom and therefore to predict the types of bonds that atoms will form. The data table shows that elements on the left side of the periodic table, groups 1, 2, and 3, have less than three electrons, which they are likely to give up. Groups 15, 16, and 17 have more than five electrons, so are likely to take electrons to fill their valence shells. Elements in group 4, which contains carbon and silicon, share electrons to make covalent compounds. The noble gases, group 18, are stable and unreactive.

Data Table	
Group on the periodic table	**Number of valence electrons**
Group 1	1
Group 2	2
Groups 3–12	1 or 2
Group 13	3
Group 14	4
Group 15	5
Group 16	6
Group 17	7
Group 18	8

Connections

Some covalent bonding produces *polar molecules*, those with a slight negative charge on one end and a slight positive charge on the other end. One such polar molecule is water. A water molecule is made of one oxygen atom and two hydrogen atoms. The nucleus of oxygen is much larger and stronger than the nuclei of the hydrogen atoms. Even though oxygen and the two hydrogen atoms are sharing electrons, oxygen pulls on them with more force than the small hydrogen atoms. As a result, the shared electrons spend more time near the oxygen end of the molecule, giving it a slight negative (-) charge. Because the electrons are pulled away from the hydrogen atoms, they have slight positive charges (+). Therefore, each water molecule is polar (see Figure 2).

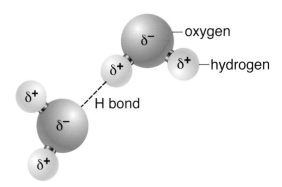

Figure 2

This polarity means that individual water molecules are attracted to each other. The attraction creates bonds that are weak, but significant. This attraction between polar molecules, called *hydrogen bonding*, is responsible for some of water's unusual properties. For example, hydrogen bonding between water molecules creates surface tension, which causes the top layer of water to have a skinlike property. Hydrogen bonds also form in many organic molecules such as proteins. In the protein in Figure 3, hydrogen bonds hold the protein in a helical shape so are responsible for the three-dimensional structure of the molecule.

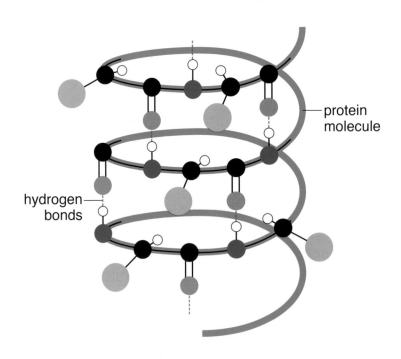

Figure 3

Want to Know More?

See appendix for Our Findings.

Further Reading

American Chemical Society. Periodic Table of the Elements. Available online. URL: http://acswebcontent.acs.org/games/pt.html. Accessed May 11, 2009. On this interactive Web page you can learn about each of the elements on the Periodic Table.

Capri, Anthony. "Water, Properties and Behavior," Vision Learning, 2008. Available online. URL: http://www.visionlearning.com/library/module_ viewer.php?mid=57. Accessed November 24, 2008. In this article Capri explains the causes and effects of surface tension.

Chem Web Online. "Introduction to Chemistry," 1997. Available online. URL: http://library.thinkquest.org/10429/high/indexh.htm. Accessed November 26, 2008. This Web site, created by students and supervised by a chemistry teacher, provides an excellent review of general chemistry concepts related to bonding.

Damelin, Dan. "Ionic and Covalent Bonds Overview," Chemsite, 2007. Available online. URL: http://chemsite.lsrhs.net/ChemicalBonds/ electronegativity.html. Accessed November 28, 2008. This Web site relates bonding to the periodic table.

19. The History of DDT

Topic

DDT is a pesticide that caused long-term ecosystem damage through biomagnification.

Introduction

Many species of insects are problematic for humans. Some are disease carriers. The *Anopheles* mosquito (Figure 1) transmits *Plasmodium*, a protozoan that causes malaria when injected into a human. Other insects feast on crops like corn and cotton. For these reasons, scientists have searched for *pesticides*, chemicals that can be used to kill troublesome insects. The first-generation pesticides were made of highly toxic chemicals, such as arsenic and hydrogen cyanide. These either proved ineffective against insects or too dangerous for humans to apply them. Second-generation pesticides were organic compounds synthesized in laboratories. In 1939, Swiss chemist Paul Muller (1899–1965) conducted experiments with 1,1,1-trichloro-2,2-bis-(p-chlorophenyl) ethane (DDT), an odorless white powder that resembles table salt. The chemical structure of DDT is shown in Figure 2. Because the chemical was widely used to kill disease-causing insects, Muller was awarded the Nobel prize in medicine and physiology in 1948.

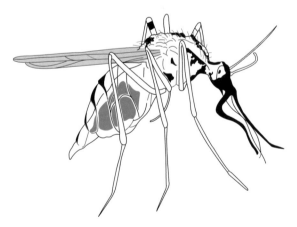

Figure 1

Anopheles mosquito

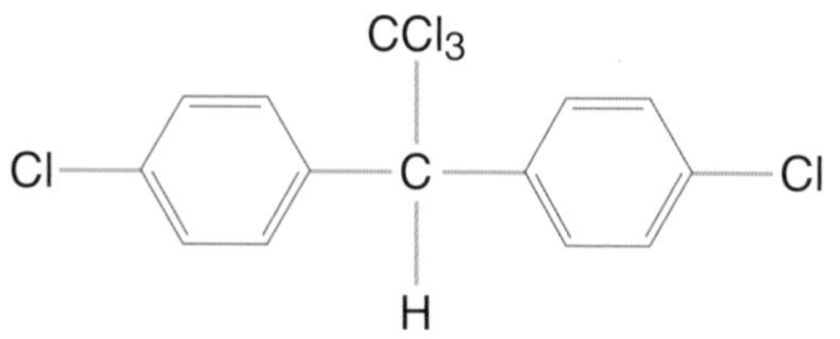

CCl₃

Cl—⟨benzene ring⟩—C—⟨benzene ring⟩—Cl

H

Figure 2

Chemical structure of DDT

Although DDT had many advantages as a pesticide, environmentally conscious scientists began to notice some problems related to the chemical. Because DDT is not soluble in water, it persists in the environment for a long time. When organisms take in DDT, the chemical dissolves in the fatty compounds in their tissues. Since animals store fat, the chemical stays with them a long time, building up as it is continuously introduced into the body through food.

Fatty compounds also make up the membranes of cells. The job of cell membranes is to control what enters and leaves cells. Because it is fat soluble, DDT can become incorporated into cell membranes, but it does not fit perfectly. As a result, the chemical damages membranes, impairing their ability to regulate the flow of *ions* into and out of the cell. This is especially problematic for nerve cells, which conduct electrical impulses by closely regulating the movement of sodium ions and potassium ions. When damaged nerve cells stop functioning, the muscles they control are no longer able to contract normally. Because of DDT poisoning, organisms die either of convulsions, erratic muscle contractions, or muscle paralysis. In this experiment, you will learn more about the effects of DDT on organisms and ecosystems.

Time Required

two 55-minute periods

Materials

- access to the Internet
- color printer (optional)
- colored pencils

- 3 sheets of plain white paper
- stapler
- science notebook

> **Safety Note** Please review and follow the safety guidelines at the beginning of this volume.

Procedure

1. Make a flip book from three sheets of plain white paper. To do so:

   a. Stack three sheets of paper so that the bottom edges are staggered with about 1/4 inch (in.) (.64 centimeters [cm]) of paper extending beyond the sheet above it (see Figure 3).

   b. Fold the top half of the papers down so that you have six staggered edges.

   c. Staple the papers at the top.

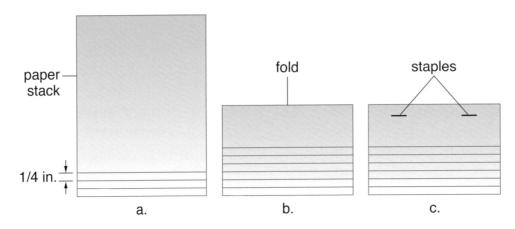

Figure 3

2. Access the Internet to find information on DDT and record your findings in your science notebook. This information will form the basis of your flip book on DDT. Also find answers to the Analysis questions.

3. Create your flip book. The top page of the flip book will be the cover page where you will place the title of the book, your name, and an appropriate drawing or photo. On the other five pages, provide information on the following topics:

   a. The advantages of DDT as a pesticide.

    b. Reasons for banning DDT.

    c. The effects of Rachel Carson's book *Silent Spring* on the public's understanding of DDT.

    d. The effects of DDT *bioaccumulation* and *biomagnification*.

    e. The effects of DDT on humans.

    Each page of the flip book should include written information and at least one picture. Make the flip book informative, interesting to read, neat, and colorful.

4. Your teacher and classmates will use the rubric to grade your flip book. Before you begin your work, look over the rubric so that you will know exactly what you are supposed to do.

Grading Rubric		
Grading criteria	**Points possible**	**Points earned**
The cover page: a. is attractive b. includes a picture c. includes a title and your name	3	
One page discusses the advantages of using DDT as a pesticide.	4	
One page explains the reasons for banning DDT.	4	
One page discusses the effects of Carson's *Silent Spring* on the public's understanding of DDT.	4	
One page explains DDT bioaccumulation and biomagnification.	4	
One page discusses the effects of DDT on humans.	4	
Each page of the book included a picture.	5	
The book was neat and well-organized.	5	
Total points	33	

Analysis

1. When was DDT first used as a pesticide?
2. Name two diseases that are spread by insects.
3. In what year was use of DDT banned in the United States?
4. How does DDT reduce bird populations?
5. Why is DDT still in use in some parts of the world?

What's Going On?

When DDT was introduced, it was considered to be a wonder chemical because it could get rid of any kind of insect pest. Farmers found that it would eliminate crop-destroying bugs, such as potato beetles, apple-eating moths, corn earworms, and cotton boll weevils (Figure 4). The peak year of use in the United States was 1959, when more than 80 million pounds (more than 36 million kilograms [kg]) of DDT were used on crops. In other countries, the use of DDT to kill malaria-causing mosquitoes and typhus-carrying body lice improved the health of millions of people. The World Health Organization (WHO) estimates that at least 25 million lives were saved by the application of this chemical. It seemed an ideal solution to insect problems because it was cheap, easy-to-use, and harmless to mammals.

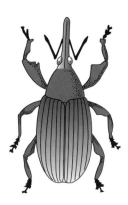

Figure 4

Boll weevil

However, by the late 1940s, some scientists were beginning to see problems. For one thing, insects were developing resistance to the chemical, so it was losing its effectiveness. In addition, DDT was found to be toxic to fish, and scientists discovered that it was accumulating in fatty tissue of other animals. DDT has a *half-life* of 8 years, which means that it takes 8 years for half of the DDT in tissue to break down. If an animal continuously eats DDT-laced food, the load of pesticide accumulates over time. Animals at the tops of *food chains*, which includes predators, like large birds and carnivorous mammals, can accumulate heavy loads of the toxin. Although the DDT does not kill these animals, it is harmful. In birds, the chemical prevents formation of strong shells on eggs, causing the deaths of all chicks. In mammals, DDT seems to mimic the action of some hormones and disrupts normal reproductive cycles. While the use of DDT was banned in 1973 in the United States and most other developed countries, the chemical is still manufactured and used routinely in some countries.

Connections

Three decades after most governments banned DDT, the chemical is showing up again in the environment. Scientists working in Antarctica found unexpectedly high levels of DDT in the body fat and the egg shells of Adelie penguins (Figure 5). After checking all regions of the penguin's environment, the source of this DDT was found to be glacial melt water. Apparently, the chemical had been carried to the poles by air currents during its peak use. Precipitation took the chemical to the surface, where it became part of the glaciers. Now, rapid warming in Antarctica due to *global warming* is causing the glaciers to melt at an unprecedented rate and releasing the dangerous chemical once again. *Krill*, tiny, shrimplike crustaceans, live in the melt water and are the primary food of penguins. Currently, scientists do not think that the birds are likely to suffer serious injury based on the amounts of the chemical they see in the melt water. However, no one knows if the melting has already hit the peak deposits of DDT.

Figure 5

Adelie penguin

Want to Know More?

See appendix for Our Findings.

Further Reading

Chem Cruising. "DDT, An Introduction." Available online. URL: http://www.chem.duke.edu/~jds/cruise_chem/pest/pest1.html. Accessed November 27, 2008. The overview of DDT provided on this Web site is the result of a cooperative effort involving teachers, students, and professional in the chemical industry.

Ehrlich, Paul R., David S. Dobkin, and Darryl Wheye. "DDT and Birds," 1988. Available online. URL: http://www.stanford.edu/group/stanfordbirds/text/essays/DDT_and_Birds.html. Accessed November 26, 2008. The authors explain shell-thinning effects of DDT on the eggs of birds.

U.S. Fish and Wildlife Services. "U.S. Fish and Wildlife Services Historic News Releases–DDT." September 24, 2008. Available online. URL: http://www.fws.gov/contaminants/Info/DDTNews.html#disclaimer. Accessed November 27, 2008. This Web site reproduces original documents from 1945 to 1998 that trace the history of problems associated with DDT.

20. The Power of a Tsunami

Topic

Tsunamis are destructive waves that endanger the lives of coastal residents.

Introduction

Just a few days after Christmas 2004, an undersea earthquake in the Indian Ocean produced a series of gargantuan waves that slammed into the coasts of 11 countries. People were washed out to sea, drowned in their homes, and slammed by water-borne debris. According to the National Oceanic and Atmospheric Administration (NOAA), more than 230,000 people lost their lives. Most of those who survived were left homeless, all of their possessions destroyed by forces never before experienced. The waves responsible for this disaster were generated by a strong earthquake near the west coast of Sumatra, an Indonesian island. The quake registered 9.0 on the *Richter scale*.

Waves generated by this quake were not ordinary ocean waves, but *tsunamis*, a Japanese term that translates as "harbor wave." The Japanese characters that "spell" tsunami are shown in Figure 1. A tsunami is a series of waves created by sudden motions of the ocean floor. The sudden motion could be caused by an earthquake or landslide. These disturbances displace large volumes of water, giving them a hard, rapid shove and propelling them into motion with tremendous energy. Tsunamis travel out in all directions from the point of disturbance, moving as fast as 600 miles per hour (mph) (700 kilometers per hour [kph]), faster than a Boeing 747. They can reach nearby coastlines in minutes and distant shores within a few hours. As a tsunami moves up on shore, it gains height and runs up on the land.

Tsunamis are very different from ordinary wind-generated ocean waves. Wind waves affect only the upper surface of the ocean and never travel more than 60 mph (96.6 kph). Ordinary waves rarely have a *wavelength*, the distance from one wave to the next, more than 1,000 feet (ft) (304 meters [m]). However, tsunami wavelengths may be 329,000 ft, (100 kilometers [km]) long. The surges produced by tsunamis may reach up to

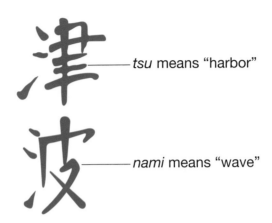

tsu means "harbor"

nami means "wave"

Figure 1

How *tsunami* is written in Japanese characters

100 ft (30 m) and have enough force to pick up cars and trucks, smash homes and businesses, and roll boulders. In this experiment, you will learn more about tsunamis and what can be done to protect coastal residents.

Time Required

45 minutes

Materials

- access to the Internet
- science notebook

Safety Note   Please review and follow the safety guidelines at the beginning of this volume.

Procedure

1. Access the National Oceanic and Atmospheric Association (NOAA) Web site, http://www.tsunami.noaa.gov/tsunami_story.html, which provides information on tsunamis and shows animations of tsunamis in action. Read this Web site and answer Analysis questions 1 through 7.

2. Access the NOAA Web site, http://www.publicaffairs.noaa.gov/ grounders/tsunamis.html. Read the material and answer Analysis questions 8 through 11.

3. Search the Internet for information on five historic tsunamis. Use the information you find to complete the data table.

4. Use what you learned in your Internet searches to write an advertisement for a local newspaper that asks people to support efforts to create and maintain an Indian Ocean tsunami warning system. In your ad, explain why the warning system is needed. Make the ad interesting and attractive.

Data Table			
Location of tsunami	Date	Loss of life	Other information

Analysis

1. What is a tsunami?
2. What are two causes of tsunamis?
3. Give an example of a tsunami produced by each of the causes in question 2.
4. What determines the height of a tsunami?
5. What determines the wavelength of a tsunami?

6. View the animation in Figure 1 of the NOAA Web site. What does it show?

7. View the animation in Figure 2 of the NOAA Web site. What does it show?

8. How are tsunamis different from ordinary ocean waves?

9. In the deep ocean, at what speed can a tsunami travel?

10. Why do tsunami waves become dangerous as they approach land?

11. Where does a tsunami's force cause the most destruction?

What's Going On?

Tsunamis are serious threats to populations living along the coasts. These gigantic waves can inundate communities, sweeping away residents, cars, and buildings within minutes. As protection, a Tsunami Warning System (TWS), supported by 26 countries, was established in 1965. The purpose of the TWS is to monitor seismic activity and wave height throughout the Pacific Ocean. The TWS evaluates data for tsunami-generating activity and provides warning information when appropriate so that coastal residents can react quickly and move to safety. NOAA and the National Weather Service operate two of the stations, one in Alaska and one in Hawaii. If the size and location of seismic activity is such that it could generate a tsunami, a warning goes out to effected coastal regions. Warning includes information on the wave's estimated arrival time and the potential wave size.

The Pacific Ocean-style warning system is not in place across the world. One reason that the tsunami of 2004 claimed so many lives is that the existing TWS does not include the Indian Ocean, a region that has seen very few tidal waves in the past. Indian officials had no way of knowing that a life-threatening wave had been generated because they lacked the equipment to gather required information. What is more, they do not have the funds to establish such a system.

Connections

Most tsunamis occur in the Pacific Ocean, primarily in the region known as the *Ring of Fire*, a geologically active zone shown in Figure 2. Earthquakes registering 7 or more on the Richter scale occur several times a year in the Pacific. The map shows the occurrence of some historically important earthquakes.

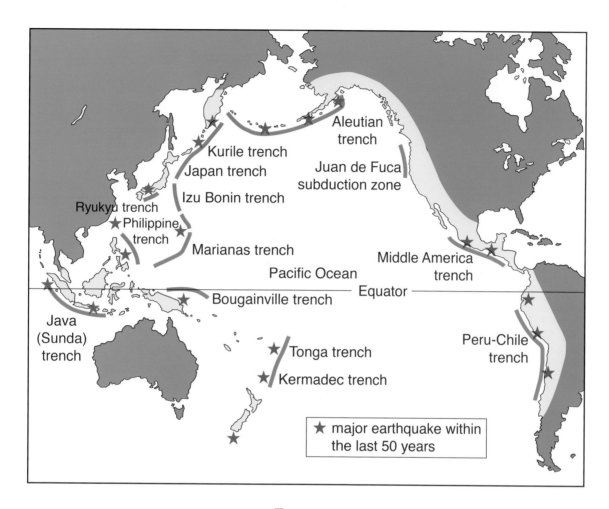

Figure 2

Ring of Fire

The Ring of Fire is located along the borders of the Pacific *tectonic plate* and several continental plates. Plates, large sections of the Earth's crust, travel slowly, moving only 1/2 to 1 inch (in.) (about 1 1/2 to 3 centimeters [cm]) each year. The plates are like giant rafts floating on the Earth's inner layer of molten *mantle*. As they travel, some plates move apart, but others scrape together or collide. In a collision, one plate is forced down underneath another. The Pacific Ring of Fire is an area where many plates are being forced downward, a process known as *subduction*. In these areas, subducted plates are pushed beneath other plates with such tremendous energy and pressure that they melt into *magma*. Figure 3 shows a plate that is moving from left to right. As it moves, it is pushed beneath another plate. Molten lava created by the subduction rises to the surface as volcanoes. This type of geologic activity to expected to continue generating tsunamis in the Pacific Ocean.

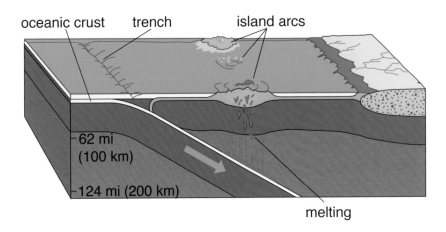

Figure 3

Want to Know More?

See appendix for Our Findings.

Further Reading

National Geographic News. "Tsunamis: Facts About Killer Waves." January 14, 2005. Available online. URL: http://news.nationalgeographic.com/news/2004/12/1228_041228_tsunami.html. Accessed November 30, 2008. This article provides general information on tsunamis and explains how tsunamis are formed.

NOAA Center for Tsunami Research. Available online. URL: http://nctr.pmel.noaa.gov/index.html. Accessed November 27, 2008. This Web site provides links to animations depicting tsunamis in various locations.

Pararas-Carayannis, George, Patricia Wilson, and Richard Sillcox. "Tsunami Warning." Available online. URL: http://wcatwc.arh.noaa.gov/book01.htm. Accessed December 6, 2008. The authors have created an entertaining, illustrated "book" that explains tsunamis.

Scope and Sequence Chart

This chart aligns the experiments in this book with some of the National Science Content Standards. (These experiments do not address every national science standard.) Please refer to your local and state content standards for additional information. As always, adult supervision is recommended and discretion should be used in selecting experiments appropriate to teaching any age group or to individual students.

Standard	Grades 5–8	Grades 9–12
Physical Science		
Properties and changes of properties in matter	5, 15	5, 15
Chemical reactions	5, 8, 16, 18	5, 8, 16, 18
Motions and forces	7, 14	7, 14
Transfer of energy and interactions of energy and matter	5, 7, 14	5, 7, 14
Conservation of energy and increase in disorder		
Life Science		
Cells and structure and function in living systems	1, 4, 8, 14, 18	1, 4, 8, 14, 18
Reproduction and heredity	1	1
Regulation and behavior	4	4

Populations and ecosystems	2	2
Diversity and adaptations of organisms	2, 12	2, 12
Interdependence of organisms	2, 3, 12	2, 3, 12
Matter, energy, and organization in living systems	2, 3, 8, 19	2, 3, 8, 19
Biological evolution	19	19
Earth Science		
Structure and energy in the Earth system	6, 9, 10, 11, 16, 20	6, 9, 10, 11, 16, 20
Geochemical cycles	3, 10, 13	3, 10, 13
Origin and evolution of the Earth system		
Origin and evolution of the universe		
Earth in the solar system	6, 17	6, 17
Nature of Science		
Science in history	5, 6, 17, 19	5, 6, 17, 19
Science as an endeavor	all	all

Grade Level

Setting

All experiments in this book must be conducted at a computer, either in a school setting or at home. In the school, the experiments can be worked on at computers in the classroom or in a computer lab, depending on availability. Students can perform the computer portion of each experiment alone or with a partner.

Whether at school or at home, adults should closely supervise students when accessing the Internet. Remind students that the ability to use of the Internet is a privilege. At school, students and their parents should sign an Internet use agreement form in which students agree to comply with the school system's rules regulating the use of appropriate Web sites. These Internet use agreements should be on file. The use of the Internet in this volume is for educational purposes only. Web sites to avoid include, but are not limited to, those that violate the law, transmit offensive messages or programs, transmit pornography in any form, or transmit games. In addition, remind students to be safe on the Internet and keep all personal information confidential. Students should never reveal their names, addresses, telephone numbers, or any other information that would enable a person to locate them.

One experiment needs access to the outdoors—in "Using Cloud Patterns to Predict Weather," students follow their teacher to an outdoor area to observe cloud shapes. When outdoors, be sure that students wear appropriate clothing for the weather and terrain and that they are supervised at all times.

Our Findings

1. BIOETHICS VIDEO PRODUCTION

Idea for class discussion: Ask students to define the term *ethics*. Lead them into a discussion about the difference between right and wrong.

Teacher notes: Some Web sites that might be useful include:

CBS News. "Building a Better Baby," http://www.cbsnews.com/stories/2007/10/21/sunday/main3389134.shtml;

Bioethics.net. http://www.bioethics.net/and Bioethics Update. http://ethics.sandiego.edu/Applied/Bioethics/index.asp.

Analysis

1. As science has expanded our options, we will face more ethical issues than citizens in the past.

2. Answers will vary.

3. Answers will vary. Some current bioethical issues ask us to answer questions that do not have simple solutions.

4. Answers will vary.

5. Answers will vary.

2. CORAL REEF CONSERVATION

Idea for class discussion: Ask students to name some of the organisms that are unique to coral reefs. Introduce the idea that reefs are unique habitats.

Analysis

1. stony coral, deep water coral, and soft coral

2. A polyp is an individual organism with a mouth, tentacles, and stomach.

3. Hundreds of thousands of corals live in the same area and connect laterally to each other with thin pieces of tissue.

4. A coral uses tentacles to capture food, which it pushes into its mouth. Wastes are expelled through the mouth.

5. Coral polyps sting their prey with nematocysts then use tentacles to bring the stunned prey into their mouths.

6. The corals provide a safe environment for the zooxanthellae, which provide food for the corals through photosynthesis.

7. Coral color is due to the presence of zooxanthellae. When corals become stressed, they expel their zoothathellae and take on a white, bleached appearance.

8. Corals contain algae, which are photosynthetic. Suspended matter in water blocks sunlight from the algae and reduces their productivity.

9. Stony coral build skeletons of calcium carbonate. Although each coral animal is small, thousands of individuals contribute to the reef.

10. b. have large, flattened branches; c. have wide plates that create whorllike patterns; d. resemble fingers; a. grow in thin layers on the substrate

11. Free swimming larvae attach to substrates on the edges of islands or continents.

12. fringing, barrier, and atoll

13. 100,000 to 30 million years

14. Reef-building corals grow best in water between 73.4 and 84.2°F (23° and 29°C) in very salty, clear water.

15. Adult corals spend their lives in one place.

16. Corals produce buds that are clones of the parents. The buds break off to form free-living adults.

17. Male and female coral broadcast their gametes in the water. Gametes unite, forming swimming planula larvae.

18. Coral reefs are the most biologically diverse marine ecosystems. They provide homes for millions of animals and may be the storehouses of future medicines.

19. In that season, 70 to 80 percent of all coral reefs in the Indo-Pacific were killed.

20. Answers will vary but could include pollution, overfishing, destructive fishing techniques, and collecting live corals to sell.

21. Answers will vary but could include dredging, coastal development, agricultural and deforestation activities, sewage treatment plants, leaking fuels, antifouling chemicals, and oil spills.

22. Human-made pollutants and increasing water temperature contribute to coral disease.

23. Coral reefs are biologically diverse ecosystems that support hundreds of different types of organisms and provide jobs for humans around the globe.

3. CARBON FOOTPRINT

Idea for class discussion: Ask students which causes more damage to the environment: a fast-food hamburger or a riding lawnmower. You can leave this question unanswered for later discussion or help them understand that all of the processes that go into making a hamburger create a lot of carbon dioxide. Remind students that carbon dioxide is a pollutant.

Analysis

1. Answers will vary.

2. Answers will vary, but the carbon footprint should be reduced by several points.

3. The Nature Conservancy helps fund alternative energy plants (such as windmills or hydroelectric dams), protect natural areas, and plant trees.

4. Patrick and his family rely on public transportation instead of a personal car. He also does most of his work electronically instead of using printed material.

5. Answers will vary but could include recycling, turning off the lights as much as possible, adjusting the thermostat to higher temperatures in the summer and lower temperatures in winter, using public transportation instead of cars, and eating locally produced foods.

6. Plants take up carbon dioxide, helping remove this greenhouse gas from the atmosphere.

7. Answers will vary. Students might suggest that the entire planet is one community and what we do on a local level affects others.

8. The Nature Conservancy is a nonprofit organization that preserves natural areas. Accomplishments that student describe will vary.

9. A compact fluorescent light bulb is a small fluorescent bulb designed to fit lamps and other devices originally designed for incandescent bulbs.

10. An incandescent bulb produces light by heating a filament until it glows. A CFL bulb causes a gas in a tube to glow.

11. If everyone replaced one incandescent bulb with a CFL bulb, we could save enough energy to light 3 million homes for 1 year and prevent emissions equivalent to 800,000 cars.

12. CFL bulbs reduce energy consumption by 75 percent and last 10 times as long as incandescent bulbs.

4. VIRTUAL FETAL PIG DISSECTION

Idea for class discussion: Ask students to give some advantages and some disadvantages of dissection. Help them understand that dissection is considered to be a critical part of training for individuals entering medical professions.

Analysis

1. anterior

2. sagittal

3. medial

4. distal

5. Female pigs have urogenital papillae.

6. Urogenital tract in males opens near the umbilical cord. Urogenital and digestive systems open into the anal region in females.

7. The nares take air into the sinuses for warming and sensing.

8. papillae. The tongue is muscular and covered with small bumps (papillae). Papillae are larger along the edges.

9. A salivary gland is found in each cheek.

10. The hard palate is made of bone and located anterior to the soft palate. Both palates are covered with mucus membranes.

11. Unerupted teeth are teeth that have not yet emerged and will develop into tusks and other teeth as the pig matures.

12. pharynx; esophagus; trachea

13. epiglottis

14. liver

15. To locate the stomach, lift the lobes of the liver.

16. about 6 ft (250 cm)

17. The small intestine digests and absorbs nutrients

18. The large intestine is darker in color. It is shorter but has a larger diameter.

19. The gallbladder is located between the lobes of the liver. It secretes bile to helps in digestion.

20. The pyloric sphincter controls the release of chyme from stomach to small intestine.

21. Rugae are folds that increase the surface area of the stomach.

22. The spleen is below and to the left of the stomach.

23. The rectum stores feces.

24. The pancreas produces digestive enzymes.

25. The mesenteries are membranes that hold the intestines together.

26. The excretory system removes metabolic wastes and drugs from the body.

27. Kidneys are located below the digestive system, beneath the peritoneum.

28. The function of kidneys is to remove metabolic wastes from blood and to help regulate water balance.

29. renal arteries; renal veins

30. ureters; urethrae

31. pericardium

32. two lungs

33. The thymus gland is located in the midsection of the neck. It helps establish the pig's immune system.

34. The coronary artery runs from the anterior to the posterior section of the heart along the midline. It carries blood to heart tissue.

35. The atria are smaller and darker than the ventricles.

36. The aorta goes over and behind the heart.

37. Left. The left ventricle pumps blood throughout the entire body. The right ventricle pumps blood to the lungs, a shorter distance.

38. right atrium

39. left atrium

40. Heart valves are located between each atrium and ventricle. They prevent blood from flowing in the wrong direction.

41. The ovaries are small, almond-shaped structures on each side of the bladder. Oviduct are thin tubes that connect the ovaries to the uterus. The uterus is a flattened sac in the pelvic region, anterior to the rectum.

42. The testicles are small masses located within the testes (held by the scrotum). The epididymae are masses of whitish tissue on the sides of the testes.

43. Air enters the nares, travels through the mouth, glottis, larynx, and trachea to the lungs.

44. 3 layers of meninges

45. olfactory lobes; pons; medulla oblongata

46. The thalamus is located in the center of the brain anterior to the medulla oblongata. Motor and sensory fibers form synapses in the thalamus, which sends impulses to and from the cerebral cortex.

5. CONSERVATION OF MASS

Idea for class discussion: Point out that Albert Einstein gave us some of our newest information on the relationship of mass and energy with his equation $E=mc^2$.

Analysis

1. 1743–94; France

2. tax collector

3. The phlogiston theory stated that in addition to the four known elements (fire, water, air, and earth), there was a fifth element called phlogiston that was found in combustible bodies. This element was released during burning.

4. Lavoisier demonstrated that burning and oxidation are similar chemical processes involving oxygen, not phlogiston.

5. Answers will vary but should include a calorimeter and a balance.

6. The law of conservation of mass states that during a chemical reaction, mass is conserved. He showed that the mass of the reactants had to equal the mass of the products.

7. Marie Anne Lavoisier kept notes, drew illustrations, and shared ideas with Antoine.

8. A chemical reaction is a change in which matter is rearranged to yield new products.

9. Bubbling and a change in temperature indicated a chemical change.

10. endothermic; The bag felt cool.

11. Answers will vary. The mass should remain the same, although small change could have occurred due to experimental error.

12. Yes. The mass of the bag at the beginning and end of the experiment was about the same.

13. Lavoisier's work showed that chemical changes did not use up or destroy matter, as did this experiment.

14. The bag must be carefully weighed to show that a change in mass did not take place.

6. ASTRONAUT TRADING CARDS

Idea for class discussion: Ask students to name some astronauts. Write these names on the board. After the activity, ask students to expand the list.

Analysis

1. An astronaut is an individual trained to travel in space.

2. Answers will vary. Scientists did not want to risk a human life until they knew that chances for survival were very good.

3. c. first U.S. astronaut in space; a. first astronaut to orbit the Earth three times; d. first person in space; b. one of the first men to walk on the Moon

4. Answers will vary but could include: fly, or assist flying, the vehicle; help maintain the vehicle; and carry out experiments or specific tasks.

5. Answers may vary. The average age is 34.

7. SIMPLE MACHINES

Idea for class discussion: Have students describe what life would be like without any machines.

Analysis

1. Work is the force multiplied by distance.

2. Force is measured in newtons, distance in meters, and work in newton meters.

3. A simple machine changes the force and distance.

4. Simple machines reduce the force required (or the direction in which the force moves).

5. The wedge group includes the inclined plane, screw, and wedge. The pulley, lever, and wheel and axle are in the lever group.

6. Mechanical advantage is the ratio of the resistance force to the effort force.

7. $$MA = \frac{F_R}{F_E} \qquad MA = \frac{d_R}{d_E}$$

    Mechanical advantage can be calculated two ways: by dividing resistance force by effort force or by dividing resistance distance by effort distance.

8. A lever is a rigid bar that rests on a fixed point called a fulcrum.

9. You push (or pull) one end of a lever to lift a weight on the other end.

10. See the figure below.

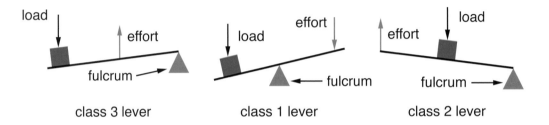

class 3 lever   class 1 lever   class 2 lever

11. A pulley is a rope or chain wrapped around a wheel that usually lifts heavy objects.

12. A pulley changes the direction of the force.

13. A fixed pulley is attached to an immovable point, such as the ceiling. A moveable pulley moves up and down with the load. A moveable pulley requires less effort force.

14. A wheel and axle is made of two circular objects of different sizes in which the wheel applies an effort force and the axle produces an output force.

15. When effort is applied to the wheel, force is increased and distance and speed decreased. When effort is applied to the axle, force is decreased and distance and speed is increased.

16. An inclined plane is a sloping surface between the horizontal and vertical surfaces.

17. An inclined plane reduces the force needed to move an object by increasing the distance

18. The MA increases. Less force is needed to move the object, but the distance increases.

19. An inclined plane is stationary while a wedge moves. The effort force is applied parallel to the slope of an inclined plane but is applied to the vertical edge of the wedge.

20. The threads of a screw are like a circular inclined plane.

21. Pitch refers to the vertical distance between two threads.

22. a. 4; b. 4.16; c. 200 N

8. HYDROLYSIS AND DEHYDRATION SYNTHESIS

Idea for class discussion: Point out that water is essential for life. One of the reasons living things need water is to make chemical reactions possible. Explain that water is involved in combining atoms to make molecules and in breaking apart molecules.

Analysis

1. Organic molecules contain carbon; inorganic molecules do not.

2. because carbon has four valence electrons

3. Dehydration synthesis is a chemical reaction that joins two molecules by removing a molecule of water.

4. Hydrolysis is a chemical reaction that breaks apart a molecule into two molecules by adding water.

5. H

6. water

7. OH

9. USING CLOUD PATTERNS TO PREDICT WEATHER

Idea for class discussion: Ask students how they would predict the weather if they had to do so. Point out the value of observing one's surroundings, including the cloud formations.

Analysis

1. Answers will vary. Sunny days have few clouds, and those present may be small and of the cumulus type or high cirrus clouds. Rainy days most likely have heavy stratus or cumulostratus clouds. Days prior to rain have primarily cumulonimbus clouds or stratus clouds.

2. Answers will vary.

3. Answers will vary based on individual experimental results.

4. Answers will vary.

5. Answers will vary but could include monitoring the wind, barometric pressure, and temperature.

10. CREATE A CLIMATOGRAM

Idea for class discussion: Ask students to describe your local climate. Have them discuss the differences in the climate and weather.

Notes to the teacher: Student climatograms (step 1 of the procedure) should include a bar graph depicting the monthly precipitation and a line graph depicting average monthly temperatures. The graph and all axes should be labeled.

Analysis

1. Answers will vary based on climate data for the area during the specific month chosen.

2. Answers will vary based on climate data collected by students and based on the climate in the area over the past year. Students should compare their short-term climatogram to the 1-year climatogram that they created.

3. Answers will vary based on climatogram data. Most likely, the data in the 1-year climatogram will be slightly different from the long-term climatogram data.

4. Data in the long-term climatogram is collected over a period of 30 years, therefore the average temperatures represent a stabilized average. Since many factors such as El Niño, La Niña, and atmospheric fluctuations, can change the climate from one year to the next, the 1-year climatogram can vary from the long-term average.

5. Answers will vary, but may include: Weather conditions can vary daily in an area due to the movement of air masses in the atmosphere. The atmosphere contains air masses, or fronts, with varying temperature and pressure. As the fronts move and collide, they bring not only warmer or cooler temperatures, but also wind, rain, and storm systems. Yearly climate can be affected by varying ocean and air currents (such as El Niño/La Niña), volcanic activity, and solar variation.

11. MAPPING LIGHTNING STRIKES

Idea for class discussion: Have students describe lightning they have seen and try to remember when it occurred (time of year; prevailing weather conditions).

Notes to the teacher: Lightning strikes do not occur continuously in the United States, so you may want to use this experiment during a period of active weather. To find out where lightning is striking, access the Web site http://www.intellicast.com/Storm/Severe/Lightning.aspx and examine the U.S. map. Make a list of the states that are experiencing the most lightning strikes. Share this list with the students when they begin this activity.

Analysis

1. Answers will vary. Lightning activity is increased when there is static electricity in an area. Static electricity can be increased due to atmospheric conditions; drier air produces more electric charges. The type of soil in an area can also influence lightning activity; for example, dry, sandy soil conducts more electricity than moist clay.

2. Student graphs should include line plots for each of the states. Each line plot should have three points, showing the number of lightning strikes during each storm. Graphs should be labeled.

3. Answers will vary depending on results. Student answers should include the area that received the most lightning strikes as well as the area that received the least.

4. Answers will vary depending on results and prediction from step 1 of the procedure. Students should tell if their results agree with their prediction from step 1 and explain why it does or does not.

5. Answers will vary depending on location chosen. Student answers should include a description of the area receiving the most lightning and an explanation of why they believe the factors described contributed to the amount of lightning. Answers may include a description of the elevation, soil type, and the amount of vegetation in the area.

12. HUMAN PARASITES

Idea for class discussion: Ask students to name some parasites of animals, humans, and plants. Discuss the fact that parasites are highly specialized organisms that require a host.

Analysis

1. Answers will vary. A host is an organism that provides food and/or a place to live for a parasite.

2. Answers will vary. Some parasites use their host's food, depriving them of nutrition. Others cause local or system allergic reactions, damage tissue such as skin or muscle, or block organs like the heart or intestine.

3. Answers will vary. Parasites that kill their hosts lose their source of food.

4. Answers will vary. Most parasites have more than one animal host, and warm, humid regions support more animal populations than cool, dry ones.

5. Global warming would extend the regions in which mosquitoes can thrive, extending the spread of malaria.

13. ROCKS AND MINERALS

Idea for class discussion: Ask students to name their birthstones. If students do not know, find the birthstones for them on the list below. Birthstone are minerals that are classified as "semiprecious."

January; garnet	July; ruby
February; amethyst	August; peridot
March; aquamarine	September; sapphire
April; diamond	October; opal
May; emerald	November; topaz
June; pearl	December; turquoise

Analysis

1. Answers will vary. Students should explain how lava might produce a rock containing a particular mineral, which could then be weathered and changed into sedimentary rock, then exposed to high heat or pressure to become a metamorphic rock.

2. A rock is a conglomerate of many minerals, while a mineral is a product of geological processes and has a particular chemical composition.

3. Answers will vary.

4. Opals are not classified as minerals because they do not have an ordered structure.

5. Answers will vary.

14. BREATHING DEMONSTRATION

Idea for class discussion: Many students have the misconception that we suck air into our lungs. Point out that air flows in and out due to a difference in air pressure.

Analysis

1. Air travels through the trachea into the bronchi. From there, it goes into the bronchioles, finally arriving in the alveoli.

2. An alveolus is a small sac at the ends of the smallest bronchioles. Gas exchange occurs at the alveoli.

3. The diaphragm is a thin muscle at the base of the chest cavity that helps change the size of the rib cage.

4. Into the lungs. When the rib cage enlarges, the lungs enlarge, and air pressure drops. Air moves from an area of high pressure to an area of low pressure

5. Out. When the diaphragm moves up, the rib cages moves downward and the space in the lungs is reduced. This increases air pressure and air moves out.

6. Boyle's law explains that a decrease in pressure results in an increase in volume.

7. Answers will vary based on students' models.

8. Answers will vary based on students' models.

9. Answers will vary based on students' models, but the model should show that air moves from areas of high pressure to areas of low pressure.

15. NANOSCALE SCIENCE

Idea for class discussion: Ask students to name some very tiny machines or devices. Point out that a new field of science is working on the molecule level and developing microscopic devices.

Analysis

1. one-billionth of a meter

2. thickness of paper, 100,000 nm; gold atom, one-third of an nm; black hair, 50,000 to 180,000 nm; hemoglobin protein, 5 nm

3. Nanoscience reveals unusual biological, chemical, and physical properties.

4. The surface area of nanoscale materials is much larger.

5. Gold nanoparticles absorb light and change it into heat.

6. Carbon nanotubes are strong, lightweight, and able to conduct electricity. They may replace metal in cars, providing strong but light-weight car frames. The nanotubes can conduct heat and electricity and may be used to protect planes from lightening strikes.

7. Fields include electronics, magnetic and optoelectronics, biomedical, pharmaceutical, cosmetic, energy, catalytic and materials, chemical-mechanical polishing, magnetic recording tapes, sunscreens, automotive catalyst supports, biolabeling, electroconductive coatings and optical fibers

8. (a) millimeters, meters; (b) 1,000,000, 10^{-3}; (c) 100, 10^{-4}; (d) 1; (e) nm; (f) nm

9. 200,000 nm

10. head of a pin

16. HOW ARE CAVES FORMED?

Idea for class discussion: Find out how many students have been caving. Ask them to recount their experiences. Point out that most tourist caves have lights and that caves are naturally very dark places. Also discuss the temperature of caves, which varies with depth. Generally, caves range from 50 to 60°F.

Analysis

1. Limestone caves are the most numerous.

2. Carbonic acid is made from rainwater as it seeps through soil and combines with carbon dioxide.

3. Rainwater seeps to the water table.

4. Carbonic acid eats away limestone.

5. These structures appear after the water table is lowered.

6. The action of moving water abrades limestone and carves out caves.

7. Wave action against weak spots in the limestone carves out openings. These sea caves typically have overhangs.

8. Hot lava flows like a river down an incline. Slow-moving lava along the sides of the flow cools first. A crust forms over the top of the flow.

The tube keeps lava warm in the center, and it continues to flow. After the tube is formed, the hot lava eventually flows out, leaving the tube.

9. Extremophiles are bacteria that live in extreme conditions.

10. hydrogen sulfide

11. The gas combines with water to make sulfuric acid, which eats away the limestone and forms cavities.

12. Onondaga was formed by chemical solution in carbonate rock, primarily limestone and dolomite.

13. The sedimentary rock was laid down when prehistoric seas covered the area. Hard body parts of animals precipitated from sea water, fell to the ocean floor, and were changed to limestone by heat and pressure. This limestone was converted to dolomite, then the seas retreated.

14. $H_2O + CO_2 \rightarrow H_2CO_3$

15. It dissolves them, creating caves.

17. SUNSPOTS AND THE SOLAR CYCLE

Idea for class discussion: Show the class a picture of the aurora borealis, or northern light. Such photographs can be found on the following Web sites: Wikipedia, http://en.wikipedia.org/wiki/Aurora_(astronomy) and Michigan Tech Aurora Page, http://www.geo.mtu.edu/weather/aurora/. Point out that the intensity and frequency of the auroras is related to sunspot activity.

Analysis

1. The Sun generates 1,023 kilowatts.

2. 9 million

3. The source of the Sun's energy is nuclear fusion.

4. 50 million years

5. 4 or 5 billion years; 100 billion years.

6. In 10 to 20 million years, the Sun will expand and envelope Earth and other inner planets. Eventually, it will contract into a cool star known as a white dwarf.

7. Sunspots are dark regions on the Sun's surface that contain strong magnetic fields.

8. Sunspots are caused by strong magnetic fields that emerge through the solar surface and allow the area to cool.

9. The average number of sunspots waxes and wanes over an 11-year period.

10. When areas of the corona become confined, they erupt into areas of gas and strong magnetic fields.

11. short, intense releases of energy that last from minutes to hours

12. areas of unipolar magnetic fields where strong solar winds flow out from the Sun's surface

13. changes in the conditions of the Sun-Earth environment

14. changes in speed or density of the solar wind, which distorts the Earth's magnetic field

15. The ionosphere reflects high-frequency communication signals, such as radio and emergency broadcasts. Space weather disrupts the ionosphere.

16. cycle 23; 2000

17. 207 in Cycle 19 in 1957

18. The ionosphere is located from 50 km to 550 km above Earth.

19. When the density of the F layer is low, only low-frequency communication waves can be transmitted. When the density is high, high-frequency waves can be transmitted.

20. Answers will vary, but probably will be one to three.

21. solar minimum

18. TYPES OF CHEMICAL BONDS

Idea for class discussion: Ask students to explain why some atoms stick together to form bonds while others do not. Lead them to understand that not all atoms can form bonds, and that bonding depends on the number and arrangement of an atom's electrons.

Analysis

1. The three basic components of atoms are protons, neutrons, and electrons.

2. Electrons are located in orbit around the nucleus.

3. outermost shell

4. 2 in shell 1; 8 in shell 2; and 2 in shell 3

5. gain, lose, or share electrons

6. An ion is an atom that has gained or lost electrons.

7. Ionic bonds are made of oppositely charged ions; covalent bonds are made by sharing electrons.

8. An electron from sodium is transferred to chlorine, creating a sodium ion and a chloride ion.

9. In both cases, the outer shells are filled.

10. The two oppositely charged particles are attracted to each other.

11. The two hydrogen atoms share their outermost electrons.

12. Each hydrogen atom will have two electrons, a full outer shell.

13. In a nonpolar covalent bond, atoms share electrons equally. In a polar covalent bond, one of the atoms attracts the shared electrons more strongly than the others. As a result, the compound has a positive end and a negative end.

14. The water molecule will have a negative charge near oxygen and a positive charge near the hydrogen atoms.

15. hydrogen bonds

16. covalent, ionic, hydrogen

17. Answers will vary.

19. THE HISTORY OF DDT

Idea for class discussion: Find out if students are familiar with pesticides and with DDT specifically. If so, ask questions to find out what they know about this chemical.

Analysis

1. DDT was first used in World War II.

2. Answers will vary but could include malaria, West Nile virus, typhus, and yellow fever.

3. 1973

4. DDT damages the shells of eggs, preventing chicks from developing and hatching.

5. DDT is inexpensive and is the only pesticide available in some third-world countries.

20. THE POWER OF A TSUNAMI

Idea for class discussion: Ask students if they remember the Indian Ocean tsunami of 2004. If so, find out what they recall. Show some photographs of the region including shots taken before and after the tsunami. Photographs can be found at many Web sites including Tsunamis. com at http://www.guardian.co.uk/gall/0,8542,1379875,00.html.

Notes to teachers: Students data tables will vary. The following is a sample data table.

Data Table			
Location of tsunami	**Date**	**Loss of life**	**Other information**
Lisbon, Portugal	1755	Thousands	Affected coasts of Spain, Portugal, and North Africa
Krakatau, Sunda Strait, near Java	August 27, 1883	36,000	90-ft (27.4-m) waves
Unimak Island, Alaska	1946	Hundreds	115 ft (35 m) waves; inspired the establishment of a tsunamis warning system
Chile	1868	25,000	90-ft (27.4-m) waves swept warships anchored off the coast of Chile 430 yd (393 m) inland
Honshu, Japan	1896	27,000	Residents were celebrating a holiday

Analysis

1. A tsunami is a set of ocean waves caused by a seismic disturbance on the ocean floor.

2. A tsunami results when a dense oceanic plate slides under a lighter continental plate, displacing a large amount of ocean water. Tsunamis are also produced by underwater landslides.

3. Sliding of plates produced the 2004 tsunami in Indonesia. Underwater landslides created the 1998 tsunami in Papua, New Guinea.

4. Vertical displacement on the seafloor determines wave height.

5. Wavelength is established by the dimensions of movements on the sea floor.

6. The animation shows the movement of plates on the seafloor and the resulting wave, which travels in all directions from the disturbance.

7. The animation shows propagation of the tsunami in 2006.

8. Tsunamis differ from ordinary ocean waves in length between peaks, which can exceed 100 miles (m) (161 kilometers [km]) and time between peaks, which can be up to 1 hour.

9. 500 miles per hour

10. The waves slow down and become compressed, gaining height.

11. The most destruction is caused near the tsunami's source because the waves have only traveled a short distance and have not lost any force as a result traveling.

Glossary

adaptation   any trait that is developed to help an organism survive in its environment

alchemist   a person who practices alchemy, an early form of science with the goal of changing metals to gold

amino acids   organic molecules that are building blocks of proteins

anthropogenic   caused by or related to the activities of humans

aquifer   underground layer of water-bearing rocks and soil that holds a considerable amount of water

arthropods   animals with jointed appendages and hard external skeletons, a group that includes spiders, insects, and shrimp

astronaut   person trained for space flight

ATP   adenosine triphosphate, an energy-carrying molecule

AZT   also called zidovudine or azidothymidine, an antiviral drug used to treat HIV

barrier reef   coral reef that is separated from the shore by a lagoon

bioaccumulation   accumulation of chemicals, such as pollutants, in the tissues of living things

biomagnification   increase in concentration of chemicals in tissues with each successive step of a food chain

biome   geographic area characterized by distinctive climate and life forms

Boyle's law   the volume of a gas varies inversely with its pressure, if temperature remains constant

cadaver   dead human body that is preserved and used for anatomical study

capillary fringe   saturated layer of soil just above the water table

carbon footprint   measure of the impact of an individual's activities based on the amount of carbon dioxide that is produced by burning fossil fuels

carcinogen   any cancer-causing agent

cave   natural underground cavity large enough for a human to enter

cecum   first section of the large intestine

cellular respiration   chemical process in which oxygen combines with glucose in cells to produce energy along with the by-products carbon dioxide and water vapor

cellulose   strong, rigid complex carbohydrate found in plants that provides support and structure

cirrus clouds   feathery, high-altitude clouds made of small pieces of ice

climate   average weather conditions in an area over a long period of time

climatogram   graph showing the elements of weather, such as precipitation and temperature, plotted against each other

Cnidaria   group that includes all of the stinging-celled animals, such as jellyfish and anemones

combustion   burning, or rapid oxidation of, fuel that produces heat energy

coronal mass ejections   explosion of hot plasma from the Sun's surface

covalent bond   type of bond between atoms in which electrons are shared

crystal   rock made from the solidification of a substance that has a regular internal atomic structure

cumulonimbus cloud   large, dark vertical cloud that produces thunderstorms

cumulus cloud   dome-shaped cloud with a flat base

diatomic   having two atoms in a molecule

disaccharide   simple carbohydrate molecule made up of two glucose molecules

ectoparasite   parasite that lives on the exterior of an organism

El Niño   recurring event in the eastern and central Pacific Ocean in which ocean surface temperatures are unusually warm, affecting weather patterns

endoparasite   parasite that lives on the inside of an organism

endothermic   of or relating to a chemical reaction that absorbs heat

energy   the ability to do work

exothermic   of or relating to an a chemical reaction that releases heat

food chain   the series of organisms in an ecosystem through which energy passes

friction   force that resists the motion of an object

genetics   the study of inheritance and the way traits are passed from one generation to the next

global warming   general increase in the Earth's surface temperature due to abnormal thickening of greenhouse gases

glucose   simple sugar that serves as the body's primary source of fuel

glycogen   complex carbohydrate that serves as a glucose-storage molecule in animal tissues

gorgorlin   a tough, complex protein that makes up the skeleton of some corals

greenhouse gases   layer of carbon dioxide, water vapor, and methane gases in the atmosphere that traps heat close to the Earth

hailstones   precipitation made of balls of ice that are formed during thunderstorms by updrafts that carry water droplets up into regions of cold air

half-life   time it takes for a substance to be reduced by half

helminthes   general term referring to any type of worm, including segmented worms, round worms, and flat worms

HIV   human immunodeficiency virus, the causative agent of AIDS, a disease passed from one person to another through body fluids

hydrogen bond   weak bond between a slightly positively charged hydrogen atom of one molecule and a slightly negatively charged atom in another molecule

hydrolysis   process of splitting a compound into smaller molecules by the addition of water

ice core   sample of ice that may contain dust or dissolved gases that is obtained by drilling into an ice sheet

igneous rock   rock formed from molten rock that has solidified

Industrial Revolution   period of rapid development in industry and technology that occurred in the early 19th century

inert   lacking the ability to interact with other substances; stable

inorganic   referring to materials that do not contain carbon

invertebrates   organisms that do not have vertebrae, or backbones, such as insects, jellyfish, and worms

in vitro fertilization   procedure in which eggs are mixed with sperm outside of the body; fertilized eggs are then implanted into the uterus

ion   a charged particle

ionic bond   chemical bond formed by the attraction of two oppositely charged ions

karst   area of limestone and other soluble rocks that is characterized by sinkholes and caves

krill   shrimplike organisms in the Arctic that feed on algae and make up an important part of the food chain

La Niña   period of colder than average ocean temperatures in the central Pacific Ocean that affects global weather patterns

magma   molten rock beneath the surface of the Earth

mammal   type of vertebrate that has hair and feeds its young with milk produced by mammary glands

mammary glands   milk-producing glands in mammals

mantle   the hot, nearly melted, layer of the Earth beneath the crust and above the core

mechanical advantage   ratio of the output force of a simple machine to the input force

metamorphic rock   type of rock formed from other types of rocks that have been changed by heat or pressure

mineral   naturally occurring, inorganic substance that has a definite chemical makeup

monosaccharide   simple carbohydrate molecule made up of one glucose molecule

mutualistic relationship   relationship in which organisms of two different species exist together for the benefit of both

nanoscale science   study of the characteristics of materials that are smaller than 100 nanometers

newton   force that is required to move a 1 kilogram mass with an acceleration of 1 meter per second squared

nimbus cloud   gray cloud that causes precipitation

noble gases   a group of inert gases that are rare in the atmosphere. The noble gases include helium, neon, argon, krypton, xenon, and radon.

octet   a group of eight electrons, a stable configuration in atoms

organic   referring to materials that contain carbon

parasite   organism that lives on the body of a host organism

peptide bond   bond that forms between two amino acids

pesticide   any chemical used to get rid of pests, such as insects, rodents, or weeds

phlogiston   substance, once believed to be present in all combustible materials, that was released by burning

placenta   organ that connects a developing fetus to the mother's uterus

pneumonia   respiratory disease caused by inflammation of lung tissue due to infection or chemical agents

pneumothorax   a condition caused by the collection of air between the chest wall and lung that can compress the lung and make breathing difficult

polar molecules   molecules that have a slightly negative charge at one end and a slightly positive charge at the other end

polysaccharide   large carbohydrate molecule made up of many glucose molecules

primary caves   caves formed at the same time as the surrounding rock

respiration   the metabolic process in which organisms break down glucose to produce energy; the process of inhaling and exhaling

Richter scale   scale used to measure the amount of energy released by an earthquake

rock cycle   continuous series of events in which rock is changed over long periods of time

secondary caves   caves formed after the surrounding rock is deposited

sedimentary rock   type of rock formed when sediments are pressed together

simple machines   machines without moving parts that apply a single force. Simple machines include the lever, pulley, inclined plane, wheel and axle, wedge, and screw

solar cycle   approximate 11-year cycle of increasing and decreasing solar activity

solar flares   eruption of solar gases from the Sun's surface

solar maximum   period of the solar cycle when solar activity is at its peak

solar minimum   period of the solar cycle when solar activity is least

speleothem   deposit of mineral in a cave, such as a stalagmite or stalactite

spicules   needlelike structures that form some skeletal support in sponges

sputum   mucus brought up from the lungs by coughing

stalactites   deposits of calcium carbonate that form structures that hang from the cave ceiling

stalagmites   deposits of calcium carbonate that form structures that rise from the cave floor

starch   complex carbohydrate formed by plants from glucose molecules

stem cells   primitive types of cells from which other, more specialized cells are formed

stoichiometry   field of study concerned with the mathematical relationships of chemical formulas and equations

stratus cloud   flat cloud that forms a uniform layer

subduction   geologic process in which one crustal plate is pushed down and under another plate

sunspot   dark spot on the Sun that is cooler than the surrounding solar surface

tectonic plate   section of the Earth's crust that moves relative to the other sections

tsunami   ocean wave produced by an undersea earthquake, landslide, or volcanic eruption

umbilical cord   structure that carries nutrients and oxygen from the mother to the fetus and removes wastes and carbon dioxide

valence electrons   electrons in the outermost energy shell of an atom

valence shell   outermost energy level of an atom that contains the valence electrons

wavelength   distance from the peak of one wave to the peak of the next wave

weathered   partially decomposed or broken down by wind and water

work   applying a force on an object that causes displacement

zone of aeration   underground region above the water table where spaces between rocks contain both water and air

zone of saturation   underground region at the water table where spaces between rocks are saturated with water

zooxanthellae   symbiotic, one-celled algae that live in the tissues of some marine invertebrates such as coral

Internet Resources

The World Wide Web is an invaluable source of information for students, teachers, and parents. The following list is intended to help you get started exploring educational sites that relate to the book. It is just a sample of the Web material that is available to you. All of these sites were accessible as of May 2009.

Educational Resources

American Chemical Society (ACS). Periodic Table of the Elements. Available online. URL: http://acswebcontent.acs.org/games/pt.html. Accessed May 11, 2009. This interactive Web page provides an opportunity to explore any element on the Periodic Table.

American Museum of Natural History. Science Bulletins, 2007. Available online. URL: http://www.amnh.org/sciencebulletins/. Accessed May 11, 2009. This Web site integrates information from many resources on topics that include coral reefs, evolution, and biodiversity.

Carbon Dioxide Information Data Analysis Center. Available online. URL: http://cdiac. esd.ornl.gov/home.html. Accessed May 11, 2009. This Web site provides information on the carbon dioxide cycle and provides links to other useful resources.

Check, Erika. "Women Get an Extra Dose of X-Chromosome Genes," BioEd Online, March 16, 2005. Available online. URL: http://www.bioedonline.org/news/news. cfm?art=1661. Accessed May 11, 2009. Check provides insight into the inheritance of genetic traits on the X chromosome.

Energy Information Administration. Energy Country Analysis Briefs. Available online. URL: http://www.eia.doe.gov/emeu/cabs/contents.html. Accessed May 11, 2009. Provided by the Department of Energy, this Web site contains energy information from countries around the world.

Exploratorium. Microscope Imaging Station. Available online. URL: http://www. exploratorium.edu/imaging_station/index.php. Accessed May 11, 2009. This Web site provides amazing microscope images and stories covering various topics from blood to planaria.

Global Climate Change. "Overview of Climate Change Research," Exploratorium, 2002. Available online. URL: http://www.exploratorium.edu/climate/primer/index. html. Accessed May 11, 2009. This Web site provides information on major climate problems that are caused by pollution.

NASA. "Visible Earth," February 25, 2008. Available online. URL: http://visibleearth. nasa.gov/. Accessed May 11, 2009. Visible Earth supplies images of Earth and animations that explain Earth processes.

NASA. "Windows to the Universe." Available online. URL: http://www.windows.ucar. edu/. Accessed May 11, 2009. NASA offers an interactive Web site that lets students explore the Earth, planets, and universe through images, animations, and data sets.

National Institute of General Medical Science. "Searching for Genetic Treasures," April, 2007. Available online. URL: http://publications.nigms.nih.gov/computinglife/ searching.htm. Accessed May 11, 2009. This Web site shows how scientists use advances in computers to analyze data that can help solve problems in genetics.

National Science Foundation. "NSF and the Birth of the Internet," July 10, 2008. Available online. URL: http://www.nsf.gov/news/special_reports/nsf-net/. Accessed May 11, 2009. Through a multimedia presentation, this Web site tracks the development of the Internet.

NeMo. NeMo Explorer. Available online. URL: http://www.pmel.noaa.gov/vents/ nemo/explorer.html. Accessed May 11, 2009. NeMo Explorer lets students experience the seafloor observatory at the Axial Seamount.

Smithsonian Institution, "National Zoological Park." Available online. URL: http:// nationalzoo.si.edu/default.cfm. Accessed May 11, 2009. This Web site provides information and pictures on mammals, birds, reptiles, and amphibians.

Stern, David P. *From Stargazers to Starships*, NASA, January 21, 2008. Available online. URL: http://www-spof.gsfc.nasa.gov/stargaze/Sintro.htm. Accessed May 11, 2009. Provided by the National Aeronautics and Space Administration, this book-on-the-Web offers information on basic astronomy, Newtonian mechanics, the Sun, and spaceflight.

U.S. Geological Survey. Earthquake Hazards Program. Available online. URL: http:// earthquake.usgs.gov/. Accessed May 11, 2009. This Web site provides information on earthquakes, seismic activity, and hazard maps.

Index